Religious Perspectives on War

Also available in the Perspectives Series:

Islamic Activism and U.S. Foreign Policy, by Scott W. Hibbard and David Little

Power Sharing and International Mediation in Ethnic Conflicts, by Timothy D. Sisk

Perspectives on Pacifism: Christian, Jewish, and Muslim Views on Nonviolence and International Conflict, by David R. Smock

Islam and Democracy: Religion, Politics, and Power in the Middle East, by Timothy D. Sisk

For more information on these and other titles published by the United States Institute of Peace Press, please visit our website: www.usip.org.

Religious Perspectives on War

Christian, Muslim, and Jewish Attitudes Toward Force

REVISED EDITION

David R. Smock

Introduction by David Little

UNITED STATES INSTITUTE OF PEACE PRESS
Washington, D.C.

UNITED STATES INSTITUTE OF PEACE
1200 17th Street NW, Suite 200
Washington, DC 20036-3011

First edition 1992, revised edition 2002

Printed in the United States of America

Library of Congress Cataloging-in-Publication Data
Smock, David R.
   Religious perspectives on war : Christian, Muslim, and Jewish attitudes toward force / David R. Smock ; introduction by David Little.–Rev. ed.
      p. cm.
   Includes bibliographical references.
   ISBN 1-929223-37-4 (pbk. : alk. paper)
      1. War–Religious aspects–Congresses. 2. Just war doctrine–Congresses. 3. Persian Gulf War, 1991–Moral and ethical aspects–Congresses. 4. Persian Gulf War, 1991–Religious aspects–Congresses. I. Title

BL65.W2 S66 2002
291.5'6242–dc21
                                                    2002068807

CONTENTS

PREFACE TO THE REVISED EDITION

The horrific terrorist attacks of September 11 thrust religion onto center stage in world affairs. The perpetrators claimed religious motivation and justification. Muslim, Christian, and Jewish leaders and analysts offered religious perspectives both on the September 11 attacks and on the American-led response. Not since the Gulf War had so much attention been given to religious reflections on a world crisis, and the religious dimensions of the crisis of 2001 surpassed those of the Gulf War.

Many Western political leaders tried to minimize the degree to which religion, and specifically Islam, was at the core of the terrorist attack in an effort to avoid having the Western reaction be interpreted as an attack on Islam. British prime minister Tony Blair went so far as to say that the events of the fall and winter of 2001 had nothing at all to do with religion. But this was surely an overstatement. The presumed mastermind of September 11, Osama bin Laden, justified the terrorist attack as a religiously sanctioned *jihad* (holy war) against the United States. In one of his videotapes he said, "These events have divided the whole world into two sides, the side of believers and the side of infidels." He called on all the world's Muslims to consider themselves at war with the world's Christians and Jews. Despite the fact that bin Laden does not have the support of most Muslims and that his interpretation of the Qur'an is heretical according to many authorities, he and his supporters nevertheless articulated religious justification for their actions.

RELIGIOUS RESPONSES TO SEPTEMBER 11

Bin Laden claimed to be speaking and acting on behalf of the *umma*— the total community of Islam. But many Islamic leaders spoke out strongly against the attacks on September 11. In Saudi Arabia, Sheikh Abdulaziz al-Alshaikh, chairman of the Senior 'Ulama, stated, "The recent developments in the United States constitute a form of injustice that is not tolerated by Islam, which views them as gross crimes and sinful acts." Chairman of the Supreme Judicial Council Sheikh Salih

Al-Luheidan said, "As a human community we must be vigilant and careful to oppose these pernicious and shameless evils, which are not justified by any sane logic, nor by the religion of Islam." The 56-nation Organization of the Islamic Conference stated, "These terrorist acts contradict the teaching of all religions and human and moral values."

President Muhammad Khatami of Islamic Iran said, "What we are witnessing in the world today is an active form of nihilism in social and political realms that threatens the very fabric of human existence. . . . Vicious terrorists who concoct weapons out of religion are superficial literalists clinging to simplistic ideas. They are utterly incapable of understanding that, perhaps inadvertently, they are turning religion into the handmaiden of the most decadent ideologies. While terrorists purport to be serving the cause of religion and accuse all those who disagree with them of heresy and sacrilege, they are serving the very ideologies they condemn. . . ."

In the United States a summit meeting for fifteen national Islamic organizations issued a statement declaring, "We reiterate our unequivocal condemnation of the crime committed on September 11, 2001 and join our fellow Americans in mourning the loss of . . . innocent civilians." The Council on American-Islamic Relations (CAIR) stated, "[T]he tragedy that occurred on September 11 can not be justified by any cause or religion. We restate our condemnation of those who committed this crime and look forward to seeing the perpetrators brought to justice." Imam Abdulajalil Sajid from the United Kingdom stated, "In my humble opinion Islam believes in a civil society based on rule of law. Anyone who creates chaos (*fitna* or *fasad*) in the society through terror can be treated as *harabi* (waging war against the society) and should be brought to justice accordingly by legal process. Islam and terrorism are contradictory terms opposed to each other. Islam condemns and rejects all forms of terror, killing without due process of law, injustice, corruption, tyranny, and oppression."

Statements by other Muslim leaders, though, contained important qualifications. The Mufti of Jerusalem, Ikrima al-Sabri, opposed the killings in New York and Washington but affirmed that suicide bombings against innocents are allowed so long as they are carried out to liberate Palestine. Similarly, other Muslim leaders have stated that while the acts of

September 11 are unjustified, the violent acts against civilians orchestrated by Hamas and Islamic Jihad in Israel don't qualify as terrorism, but as legitimate responses to Israeli occupation and oppression. Yusuf Qaradawi, a widely respected Islamic scholar based in Qatar, stated, "We refuse terrorism but don't consider it terrorism to defend one's own home."

Despite these condemning statements by many prominent Islamic leaders, other Islamic leaders have given tepid responses. Some commentators explain this by noting the reluctance of Islamic leaders in the Middle East to offend fundamentalist groups. John Esposito, an expert on Islam at Georgetown University, explained, "Do you get involved in this tricky minefield when you've got to live and function within your society, which often is not just authoritarian, but depending on where you are, can be violent? . . . To speak out against violence and terrorism is something that many clerics want to do, but they also worry that their statements would be used by others, like the Bush administration, to apply to conflicts in which they see violence as legitimate [like Israel]."[1]

Christian and Jewish reactions to the events of September 11 were unequivocal. Some liberal Christian commentators sought to understand the motivations behind the attack in terms of American support for Israel, sanctions against Iraq, and the stationing of American troops in Saudi Arabia. But even that quest for understanding did not blunt the condemnation of the attacks themselves. Liberal theologian and activist Jim Wallis wrote, "[W]e must carefully distinguish between seeing global injustice as the cause of terrorism and understanding such injustice as the breeding and recruiting ground for terrorism. Grinding and dehumanizing poverty, hopelessness, and desperation clearly fuel the armies of terror, but a more ideological and fanatical agenda is its driving force." He went on to say, "The root of the terror attacks is not a yearning for economic justice for the poor and oppressed of the world. It is rather a radical rejection of the values of liberty, equality, democracy, and human rights—and the ambition of a perverted religious fundamentalism for regional and global power."[2]

In his World Day of Peace Message Pope John Paul II wrote, "When terrorist organizations use their own followers as weapons to be launched against defenseless and unsuspecting people, they show clearly the death-wish that feeds them. . . . Violence is added to violence in a tragic sequence that exasperates successive generations, each one inheriting the hatred which divided those that went before. Terrorism is built on contempt for human life. It is a profanation of religion to declare oneself a terrorist in the name of God, to do violence to others in his name."

One Christian commentator condemned the attack but sought to ensure that we don't think terrorism is the exclusive preserve of Islam. Kelton Cobb wrote, "If we are honest, we must admit that Islam, Christianity, Judaism, Buddhism, Hinduism, Sikhism—all religions—promote violence just as surely as they promote peace and justice. . . . Pacifism and terrorism are not central to the religions we know. But neither are they alien intruders. They are elements that genuinely belong to the religious traditions out of which they grow."[3]

Some Jewish leaders have seen in the events of September 11 an opportunity to convince the American public that all terrorism is cut from the same cloth and that the American outrage over September 11 should be equally strong against Palestinian terrorism against Israelis. Moreover, the armed American response to September 11 should be equated to Israel's response to Palestinian terrorism.

CHRISTIAN PERSPECTIVES ON U.S.-LED MILITARY ACTION IN AFGHANISTAN

The responses of Christian leaders to the U.S.-led military action in Afghanistan can be grouped into those adopting a just war perspective, a just peace perspective, and a pacifist position. Those advocating a just war position find military responses acceptable under carefully delimited conditions. The just peace position condones a military response only under the most extreme circumstances, and the pacifist position never accepts military action. Detailed definitions of each of these positions are provided later in the text.

Just War Perspectives

Most Christian commentators were satisfied that the U.S.-led military action in Afghanistan satisfied just war criteria. Pope John Paul II stated in his World Day of Peace message that there exists a right to defend oneself against terrorism. But he went on to assert that this right must be exercised with respect for moral and legal limits in the choice of ends and means. The guilty party must be clearly identified, and culpability cannot be extended to a whole nation, ethnic group, or religion to which the terrorists may belong. Moreover, political, diplomatic, and economic means must also be employed, including a commitment to relieving situations of oppression and marginalization that terrorists exploit. Although the Pope justified military defense, he also advocated forgiveness, and he emphasized the importance of resolving the Arab-Israeli conflict.

The U.S. Conference of Catholic Bishops issued "A Pastoral Message: Living with Faith and Hope after September 11," which also justified the restrained use of force. "The dreadful deeds of September 11 cannot go unanswered. We continue to urge resolve, restraint, and greater attention to the roots of terrorism to protect against further attacks and to advance the global common good. Our nation must continue to respond in many ways, including diplomacy, economic measures, effective intelligence, more focus on security at home, and the legitimate use of force. . . . A successful campaign against terrorism will require a combination of resolve to do what is necessary to see it through, restraint to ensure that we act justly, and a long-term focus on broader issues of justice and peace." The statement explicitly advocated adherence to just war principles of non-combatant immunity, proportionality, right intention, and probability of success. Moreover, it called for a serious effort to promote peace, which entails addressing the Israeli-Palestinian conflict, the suffering of people in Iraq, the lack of participation in political life in many Muslim countries, the abuse of human rights, endemic corruption, and grinding poverty amidst plenty, all of which terrorists exploit for their own ends.

The president of the Southern Baptist Convention's Ethics and Religious Liberty Commission, Richard Land, stated, "I don't have the right to seek vengeance or hate anyone. My government, however, has a divinely ordained obligation to exact justice from perpetrators of evil." Land pointed to scriptural support for just war theory in Romans 13:4, where "God established the state to 'bear the sword,' that is, to use lethal force to keep the peace and maintain justice."[4]

Other analysts identified unusual features of the campaign against terrorism. Martin Cook, professor of ethics at the U.S. Army War College, noted that just war theology is premised on a conflict between states. Yet the primary conflict in this case has been with al Qaeda, a non-state actor lacking the centralized authority that would make it capable of surrender, of negotiating terms, or of exercising effective control over its surrendered forces to ensure respect for cease-fires and surrender. He concluded that the challenge is "to retain the core moral elements of the just war tradition, even as we acknowledge that they must be rethought, adapted, and extended to cover our genuinely novel strategic situation."[5]

James Johnson of Rutgers University noted that modern technology and strategy, with computerized missiles and "smart bombs," can help the U.S. military adhere to just war principles, particularly the injunctions for proportionality and against civilian deaths. But Johnson and other analysts have pointed out that what may be a just war against al Qaeda in Afghanistan would not necessarily be a just war if carried over to Iraq and other targets not specifically linked to al Qaeda.[6]

Just Peace Perspective

Bishops of the United Methodist Church issued a pastoral letter in early November 2001 that expressed particular concern for protecting those who are innocent and most vulnerable and for alleviating the conditions that breed terrorism. Although the United Methodist Church has not officially declared its opposition to all war, this letter comes close to that. "We, your bishops, believe that violence in all of its forms and expressions is contrary to God's purpose for the world. Violence creates fear, desperation, hopelessness, and instability. We call upon the church to be a community of peace with justice and to support individuals and agencies all over the world who are working for the common good for all of God's children. We also call upon the church to study and work toward alleviating the root causes of poverty and other social conditions that are exploited by terrorists."

The General Assembly of the National Council of Churches of Christ in the USA called "for an early end to the bombing campaign and for all parties to collaborate with the international community to discern non-violent means that may be available by which to bring to justice those who terrorize the nations of the world." Moreover, "it is time for us as an ecumenical community to make a renewed commitment to a ministry of peace with justice, and to make real in these days the call of Jesus, 'Love your enemies and pray for those who persecute you' (Matthew 5:14–16)."

The officers of the United Church of Christ warned against meeting violence with violence. They also cited American culpability for some of the conditions that nurture terrorism. "We have grave reservations about a large-scale military response to terrorism. . . . In recent years, military campaigns in countless places have destroyed lives and threatened a whole generation of children while leaving in place oppressive regimes. Short-term solutions have sown the seeds of future catastrophe as we ally ourselves with the enemies of our enemy, only to discover that we have fed and armed those who would terrorize the innocent. . . . We must confess that we have contributed to the poverty, the militarism, and the regional instability that provide hospitable environments and comfortable havens for those who resort to violence."

Pacifist Response

The Church of the Brethren, the Mennonites, and the Quakers who collectively constitute the so-called peace churches made explicitly pacifist declarations. On September 13 the general secretary of the General Board of the Church of the Brethren called on members of her denomination to "remember who we are and whose we are. . . . This is a time to stand by our belief as Christians that all war is wrong." A number of Quaker organizations issued a Call for Peace "challenging those whose hearts and minds seem closed to the possibility of peaceful resolution," and pleading for "people of goodwill the world over [to] commit to the building of a culture of peace." The Peace and Justice Committee of the Mennonite Church USA declared that, instead of bombing and other forms of violence, "God calls us to give bread to our enemies," to do the "unexpected [in order] to stop the cycle of revenge."[7]

Christian pacifists like John Paul Lederach advocated nonviolent alternatives to military action. Lederach's alternative strategy included making every effort through law enforcement to bring the terrorist criminals to justice; energetically pursuing peace between Israelis and Palestinians; investing in a broad social agenda in the countries surrounding Afghanistan; addressing with Arab countries the root causes of internal discontent; and promoting ecumenical engagement to create a web of ethics for the new millenium. "We need to think differently about the challenges of terror. We must not provide the movements we deplore with gratuitous fuel for self-regeneration, fulfilling their martyr-based prophecies."[8] Christian pacifist theologian Walter Wink argued that we must turn the other cheek, as Jesus taught, not in weakness, but in a nonviolent attempt to resolve this crisis. The U.S. should treat this as a police action against criminals, in which the nations of the world attempt to apprehend, try, and incarcerate the perpetrators. "Can we together agree that retribution is not the way of Jesus? Can we remain steadfast in nonviolence, despite the skepticism of those who embrace violence as a way of fighting violence? . . . Christians must behave as Christians no matter how much our society and churches ridicule nonviolence as idealistic and ineffective. If we cannot be faithful in such a crisis as we presently face, when will we?"[9]

JEWISH RESPONSES

Jewish scholars and leaders were largely supportive of the U.S.-led military action in Afghanistan and as a consequence they have generally not demonstrated the kind of agonized soul searching that took place among Christian leaders. The responses of several commentators were strongly influenced by their perception that the September 11 attacks were in part attacks on Jews, Judaism, and Israel. Rabbi Eric Yoffie, president of the Union of American Hebrew Congregations, stated, "Let us make no mistake about the dangers we face. Islamic radicalism is the Nazism of our day. Like German Nazism, it rejects reason, worships death, and abhors freedom; it, too, has a blazing belief in violence and is consumed by hatred of Jews and Judaism." He then expressed support for the U.S.-led military action. "This is America's war, and Canada's war, and the war of democratic countries everywhere; it is also the war of the Jewish people. And it will not be won by appeasement, compromise, or social work. It will be won by hunting down and destroying those who seek to destroy us. . . . The war against terror must continue beyond Afghanistan and beyond bin Laden, and it must be won. . . . This war is Israel's war no less than it is ours. Fascist terror with a radical Islamic face wants to erase Israel from the map. . . ." He then said that Israelis need to be assured that America's fight against terror is universal and will oppose terrorist murder when the victims are Jews in Haifa and Jerusalem as well as Americans in New York and Washington. Moreover, Israel should not be scolded for overreacting when it defends itself against terrorist attacks.

Both the American Jewish Committee (AJC) and the Jewish Council for Public Affairs issued strong statements of support for the military initiatives President Bush took in October 2001. The AJC went on to urge President Bush to "include at an early stage in the war against terrorism the targeting of groups with a record of terrorism against Americans, Israelis, and Jewish communities." On a later occasion the executive director of the American Jewish Committee, David Harris, said, "There is such a thing in human nature as unadulterated evil. Left unchallenged, that evil can wreak unimaginable death and destruction. In the face of such evil, therefore, the politics of appeasement, the culture of moral equivalency, and the spirit of so-called forgiveness are not only doomed to failure but, even worse, can serve as recipes for self-destruction." An opinion survey conducted by the American Jewish Committee in November and December 2001 indicated overwhelming support among American Jews for U.S. military action in Afghanistan (91 percent) and strong support (69 percent) for the United States mounting a broader war against all terrorist groups and the nations that support them.

Other Jewish commentators offered more measured responses. Rabbi David Saperstein, director of the Religious Action Center of Reform Judaism, declared the war against terrorism to be a just war with a just cause under Jewish moral and legal norms. But as the war got underway in October 2001 Sapersetein said that how the war was prosecuted and whether it met the criteria for "just means" remained to be seen. He warned against an American reaction which abrogated moral principles and the Geneva Conventions. He said that the oldest laws of warfare in Western tradition are found in Genesis, where God gives man jurisdiction over his creation, including the responsibilities of punishing wrongdoers and the obligation to be merciful.[10]

Rabbi Michael Lerner, editor of *Tikkun* magazine, warned against an exclusive reliance on a military response and called for a moral transformation. "We should have learned from the current phase of the

Israel-Palestinian struggle, responding to terror with more violence, rather than asking ourselves what we could do to change the conditions that generated it in the first place, will only ensure more violence against us in the future. . . . [T]he best way to prevent these kinds of acts is not to turn ourselves into a police state, but turn ourselves into a society in which social justice, love, and compassion are so prevalent that violence becomes only a distant memory."

Rabbi Arthur Waskow, director of the Shalom Center, wrote on his website, "The lesson is that only a world where we all recognize our vulnerability can become a world where all communities feel responsible to all other communities. And only such a world can prevent such acts of rage and murder. If I treat my neighbor's pain and grief as foreign, I will end up suffering when my neighbor's pain and grief curdle into rage. But if I realize that in simple fact the walls between us are full of holes, I can reach through them in compassion and connection. Suspicion about the perpetrators of this act of infamy has fallen upon some groups that espouse a tortured version of Islam. Whether or not this turns out to be so, America must open its heart and mind to the pain and grief of those in the Arab and Muslim worlds who feel excluded, denied, unheard, disempowered, defeated."

ISLAMIC PERSPECTIVES

Although Islamic criticism was often muted in the case of Muslim leaders in countries officially supporting the United States, most other Islamic pronouncements were critical of the U.S. actions. A National Muslim Leadership Summit held in Washington in October 2001 declared, "We believe the bombing in Afghanistan is not in the long-term interest of our country or the world at large. The bombing victimizes the innocents, exacerbates the humanitarian disaster, and creates widespread resentment across the Muslim world. Allowing thousands of innocent civilians to die in the harsh Afghan winter will only serve to weaken the global resolve to root out terrorism. The senseless starvation of women and children will fuel hate and extremism. . . . As American Muslims, we stand ready to help our government in building bridges of understanding with Muslim countries, and assist in removing root causes of misunderstanding grievances and conflict." The summit also strongly condemned the prospect of the United States attacking other Muslim states, a viewpoint shared by Muslim leaders worldwide. The statement asserted that such attacks would aggravate "an already explosive and destabilizing situation."

The Islamic Circle of North America called for the United States to extend its desire to bring terrorists to justice by addressing other cases of severe injustice. "The Palestinians have been seeking justice for more than half a century. . . . People in Chechnya, Iraq, Uzbekistan, and several other places across the world are suffering the horrors of state terrorism on a daily basis. . . . If we are to seek a lasting peace for this world, we must address these structural imbalances that perpetuate such unjust and oppressive systems."

Muqtedar Khan of Adrian College wrote that the United States should stop "obsessing over bin Laden and Islam and examine the recent history of their actions overseas to grasp the depth of hatred they engender among foreigners." Moreover, "when the United States responds to the murder of innocent people with massive attacks that kill more innocent people, then they are merely responding to terror with terror."[11]

The most extreme condemnation of American actions came from radical clerics like Sheikh Hamoud al-Shuaibi in Saudi Arabia who considered U.S. military action to be a war against Islam and Muslims worldwide. He called for a *jihad* against the United States. "It is the duty of every Muslim to stand up with the Afghan people and fight against America. . . . Everyone who supports America against Islam is an infidel, someone who has strayed from the path of Islam."[12] Shuaibi and other radical clerics have considerable influence and large popular followings in Saudi Arabia, largely because of the misgivings of many Saudis about their country's ties to the West and about the behavior of the kingdom's royal family.[13] Despite this, only a tiny fraction of clerics from Saudi Arabia or from other Muslim countries issued statements similar to Shuaibi's.

A carefully selected survey of American Muslims conducted by Zogby International in November 2001 indicated that President Bush earned an overall 58 percent approval rating on his handling of the attacks on

September 11. Two-thirds agreed with the Bush administration assertion that the war was being fought against terrorism, not Islam. But despite this approval, three-fifths believed the attacks could have been prevented, almost two-thirds believed the military effort could lead to further terrorist attacks, and over two-thirds said the military effort could lead to a more unstable Middle East. Half of the American Muslims surveyed supported the military action against Afghanistan, while 43 percent opposed it. Over three-fourths said that American foreign policy in the Middle East led to the attacks, while two-thirds suggested that a change in America's policy in the Middle East would be the best way to wage the war against terrorism.

How Does the War in Afghanistan Compare to the Gulf War?

Much of the volume that follows, first published in 1992, is a broad consideration of religious perspectives on war. Some parts, however, relate specifically to the Gulf War. Hence it is worth reflecting on the parallels and differences between the war in Afghanistan and the Gulf War.

One important parallel is that both wars involved Western and Muslim states. As a consequence, religious differences automatically came into play. In the case of the Gulf War, Saddam Hussein called for a *jihad* against the Western "invaders." But this attempt to invoke a religious sanction was not taken seriously by most Muslims, since Saddam Hussein had invaded another Muslim country and because few took his religious declaration to be genuine or convincing. But al Qaeda and the Taliban in Afghanistan both declared themselves to be Islamic purists. Osama bin Laden called for a war by Muslims against Christians and Jews and more particularly against the United States. Thus, a warped religious motivation was central to the terrorist attacks on New York and Washington, and the U.S.-led attack on Afghanistan provoked a virulent response among Islamic fundamentalists.

Both conflicts precipitated religious commentary. But American public opinion was more deeply divided in the case of the Gulf War and this provoked a more vigorous public debate on the morality of American action in the Gulf. Just war principles were widely invoked, both by supporters and opponents of U.S. military action. Even the president sought to defend U.S. action in the Gulf by declaring the American intervention to be consistent with just war principles.

The application and fulfillment of just war principles differed in the two cases. The just cause for U.S. military retaliation was clearer and less frequently challenged in the case of al Qaeda/Taliban than the Gulf War. But as explained earlier, since al Qaeda is a non-state actor and just war criteria were designed to apply to wars between states, the just war criteria were not as convincingly applicable in Afghanistan as they were in the Gulf War. While civilian casualties were central issues for critics in both cases, the enhanced precision of U.S. weapons meant that civilian casualties were not as widespread in Afghanistan as they were in Iraq.

Analysts of both conflicts have tried to explain them by citing what John Kelsay refers to in this book as "historical thickness." While the immediate cause of the Gulf War was the invasion of Kuwait by Iraq, a full exploration of the causes would have to include the fact that the United States helped arm Iraq during the Iran-Iraq war in the 1980s, as well as other factors going back to Ottoman imperialism. In the case of al Qaeda and Afghanistan, analysts have noted such factors as the provision of arms and military training by the United States for the mujaheddin (including al Qaeda) fighting the Soviets in Afghanistan in the 1980s, the U.S. military presence in Saudi Arabia, and long-term American support for Israel.

What was evident after the Gulf War and became even more compelling in the al Qaeda/Afghanistan aftermath is how important it is for religious leaders from the three Abrahamic traditions—Christianity, Judaism, and Islam—to engage in regular and deep dialogue with each other. They need to share perspectives and learn from each other. They can enrich each other's understanding of international conflicts and appropriate responses, particularly when religion is a precipitating factor. Interfaith dialogue can also deepen the comprehension by each faith community of issues surrounding peace and justice. As became evident in the discussion which led to the original publication of this book, interaction among the three traditions regarding the complex ethical dilemmas of war and peace leads to mutual enrichment.

THE REVISED EDITION

This new edition of *Religious Perspectives on War* reprints the text of the first edition in full. The new preface (above) describes in some detail the differences and similarities between the Gulf War and the war against al Qaeda/Taliban. We have also made a few tyographical corrections in the text, and we have updated the "Suggestions for Further Reading," almost doubling its length. Otherwise, the text remains the same. Note, for example, that we have not attempted to update the biographies of symposium participants, and their affiliations may have changed.

NOTES

1. Quoted in Douglas Jehl, "Speaking in the Name of Islam," *New York Times*, December 2001, Week in Review, p. 1.

2. Jim Wallis, " A Light in the Darkness," *Sojourners*, November–December 2001, p. 9.

3. Kelton Cobb, "A Season of Violence," http://macdonald.hartsem.edu/cobbl.htm, p. 3.

4. "Religious Leaders Contemplate 'Just War.'" www.usatoday.com, September 27, 2001, p. B9.

5. Martin L. Cook, "Terrorism and 'Just War': Moral Challenges," *Christian Century*, November 14, 2001, pp. 22–23.

6. Bill Broadway, "Challenges of Waging a 'Just War'" *Washington Post*, October 13, 2001, p. B9.

7. William Vance Trollinger Jr., "Peace Churches Make a Witness: Nonviolent Voices," *Christian Century*, December 12, 2001, pp. 18–22.

8. John Paul Lederach, "Giving Birth to the Unexpected," *Sojourners*, November–December 2001, p. 23.

9. Walter Wink, "The Silence of God," *Sojourners*, November–December 2001, p. 28.

10. "Religious Leaders Contemplate 'Just War,'" www.usatoday.com, September 26, 2001.

11. *Islamic Perspectives on Peace and Violence*, Special Report, United States Institute of Peace, January 24, 2001.

12. Douglas Jehl, "For Saudi Cleric, Battle Shapes Up as Infidel vs. Islam, *New York Times*, December 5, 2001, p. B1.

13. Ibid, p. B4.

A NOTE TO READERS

On March 19, 1992, the United States Institute of Peace sponsored a daylong symposium in Washington, D.C., that brought together twenty-four Christians, Muslims, and Jews to discuss religious attitudes toward the use of force in international affairs. Their discussion was prompted by the Gulf War, which had ended little more than a year before. However, although the Gulf War provided the symposium's starting point, conversation soon began to range throughout history, across faiths, and deep into abiding theological and moral questions.

This publication presents a report of that symposium, a report that captures the broad spectrum of opinions offered and the wide-ranging debate they inspired. While this book offers much food for thought to religious scholars, it is also intended to be read and understood by general readers—people for whom the Gulf War may have kindled or reignited an interest in the relationship between religious ethics and the use of force.

An introduction by the Institute's senior scholar, David Little, sets the stage for the following discussion, highlighting the issues that animated discussion and explaining the evolution and content of the just war doctrine, a doctrine which received much attention during the symposium. The report on the symposium lends itself to use as curriculum in classroom discussions on war and peace. Church groups and other citizen and community associations will also find the report an informative and stimulating source for debates on the use of force. A glossary of terms and a suggested reading list supplement the text.

The United States Institute of Peace is pleased to have encouraged interfaith dialogue on this important subject and hopes that readers will find in this book much that will deepen their understanding and inspire their continuing reflection on religious and ethical attitudes toward the use of force in international affairs.

INTRODUCTION

DAVID LITTLE
Senior Scholar
United States Institute of Peace

Religion was an important part of the Gulf War experience. Differences among Muslims, Christians, and Jews were a sensitive matter, provoking debate and raising hackles not only among soldiers and civilians within the war zone but also among politicians and publics watching from farther afield. In addition, religious leaders in the Middle East and the West played a significant role in shaping public discussion, and they also attracted considerable media attention by passing judgment on the war. Conflicting pronouncements by Muslim clerics reflected divisions within the Islamic community over whether the war against Saddam Hussein was justified, and Saddam himself made copious use of anti-Western statements by some Muslim officials.

For their part, Christian authorities weighed in on various sides of the public debate in the West. Some Protestant and Catholic leaders in Europe and America defended the allied action according to "just war doctrine"—that set of standards long employed by Christians and others for appraising the use of force. President Bush and members of his administration applied these arguments in their own defense of Operation Desert Storm.

But there were contrary views. Some Christian critics argued that the allied effort in the Gulf did not meet the standards of justifiable force, while others claimed that the standards are by now irrelevant because of modern conditions and instruments of war. Pacifist critics contended that from a Christian point of view force is incapable of resolving conflict.

Nor were Jewish leaders silent. Particularly those in Israel took strong exception to Muslims and Christians who challenged the allied effort. With Jewish survival seemingly under serious threat from Saddam Hussein, the validity of military defense could, for Jews, hardly be doubted.

These different currents and cross-currents of religious opinion concerning the use of force need sorting out and clarifying. The occasion for doing so was provided by the variety of religious responses to the chain of events that followed Iraq's invasion and occupation of Kuwait on August 2, 1990. But the implications extend beyond the Gulf War.

Such clarification should help us better understand why religious responses to conflict vary so widely, as well as whether there is any common ground for modifying the differences. An interfaith setting is not only vital to this process but also offers an opportunity to extend and expand the conversation begun by Muslims, Christians, and Jews during the Gulf War.

The object of the exercise is not simply to encourage religious communities to tidy up and, where possible, to coordinate their discourse concerning matters of war and peace. Since religiously inspired discussion of the Gulf War had such a major impact upon public reflection, it seems likely that efforts by the religious communities to clarify their attitudes toward force will raise the level of general public understanding as well.

Toward encouraging such clarification, the United States Institute of Peace sponsored a daylong symposium on March 19, 1992, entitled, "Religious Perspectives on the Use of Force After the Gulf War." Twenty-four individuals (sixteen Christians, four Muslims, and four Jews) of varying affiliations and representing a broad range of opinions participated.

The symposium resulted in a frank airing of differences among Christians, Jews, and Muslims, all in a remarkable spirit of civility and mutual respect. Areas of common interest emerged that can serve as a basis for continuing conversation. The report on the symposium presented in the following pages confirms the value of "multilogue" among people of different opinions and perspectives.

JUST WAR FOCUS

Most of the symposium discussion centered on the just war standards that played a prominent role in Western public debate over the Gulf War. While by no means all Christian participants in the symposium, let alone all Jewish and Muslim participants, regarded just war standards in the same way, these standards nevertheless served to focus central points of controversy concerning the use of force. Moreover, although just war standards are historically associated with Christianity, the discussion revealed some interesting parallels in the Jewish and Islamic traditions, suggesting some basis for common ground among the three Abrahamic faiths.

The Evolution of Just War Standards

The story of the connections between just war standards and the Christian church is complicated. Christians did not invent the idea that lethal force wants regulating. Many "pagan philosophers," like Aristotle and Cicero, believed that society is impossible without the just administration of force. As a matter of fact, Christians came rather late to such concerns. In their early days, Christians stood on the margins of society, altogether turning their backs on force and following what was for them the central message of peace and nonviolence of their martyred Lord. That emphasis has continued ever after to inspire Christian pacifists.

Not until the fourth century A.D., when Christianity became the established religion of the Roman Empire, did Christians begin to assume a sense of responsibility for the conduct of public affairs, and, most especially, for the way force is administered inside the borders of a state or empire, as well as in foreign conflicts. Saints Ambrose and Augustine led the way by recovering pre-Christian teaching and reshaping it into what came to be known as "Christian just war doctrine." It is, to be sure, a doctrine in only the loosest sense, for it has been variously revised over the centuries, and to this day, is open to quite diverse interpretation.

If just war doctrine deviated from the pacifism of the early church, it also stood against an opposing tendency in the Biblical tradition in favor of the "holy war" or "crusade," which features the unrestricted use of force in God's service. The instances of unrestrained warfare mentioned, for example, in the book of Deuteronomy occasionally inspired some Christian groups to believe that an exercise of violence can in itself be a sacred calling. For just war advocates, by contrast, force is sometimes necessary, but it is always dangerous and must be restrained. Atrocities committed in the name of the Lord are atrocities nevertheless.

Because force is potentially so dangerous, so likely to become arbitrary, any decision in favor of using it must bear a heavy burden of proof. Accordingly, just war standards have come to be worked out in response to four basic questions:

1. Who has the authority to order that force be used?
2. What are the reasons (causes) necessary and sufficient for such an order?
3. What special, additional considerations ought to govern the decision to employ force?
4. What is acceptable conduct, under conditions of armed conflict, in respect both to armed antagonists and to unarmed bystanders?

Five standards have been developed in response to the first three questions, and two standards in response to the fourth question. (Although they are not the only standards that have appeared in the tradition, these seven have by now achieved widespread acceptance.)

The first group concerns the conditions for deciding to use force. It is known as "justice on the way to war," or *jus ad bellum*. The second group concerns the conditions governing the conduct of combat, or the actual use of force. It is known as "justice in the midst of war," or *jus in bello*.

Jus ad Bellum   *Justice on The Way to War*

Legitimate Authority. Requiring that only duly selected or otherwise legitimate officials may decide to resort to force is one way of protecting against arbitrariness in these matters. Everything depends, of course, on *which* theory of political legitimacy is adopted. A monarchist and a constitutional democrat would have conflicting attitudes toward rightful authority. As a matter of fact, the Christian church was for a long time divided, not only over political theory, but also over whether ecclesiastical authorities, in addition to civil officials, might properly certify force.

Just Cause. On the assumption that force employed without good reason is an egregious violation, only certain reasons qualify as justifications for going to war, though they, too, are subject to some variation. The three standard reasons are self-defense, recovery of stolen assets, and punishment of wrongdoing. Probably because it is less susceptible to abuse, self-defense has in modern times gained a certain priority. There again, the Christian tradition has sometimes been at odds with itself, not only in regard to applying the three so-called temporal justifications for using force, but also in regard to whether there are bona fide religious reasons for going to war, such as license to correct apostasy in another country.

Peaceful Intention. According to Aristotle, "we wage war in order to have peace," and therefore using force for any other purpose than to restrain and minimize force is reprehensible. This standard draws attention to the fact that a primary objective of just war doctrine is the pursuit of a just peace. Consequently, actions involving force must be judged by the contribution they make to resolving rather than intensifying conflict.

Last Resort. Before force may justifiably be used, all reasonable attempts at peaceful resolution of a conflict, including negotiation, mediation, and so on, must be exhausted. Along with peaceful intention, this standard signals the presumption in favor of peace that undergirds just war doctrine. To be sure, one of the traditional difficulties of applying this standard has been finding a way to ascertain when the search for peaceful resolution may acceptably give way to the use of force.

Reasonable Hope of Success. This is a counsel of prudence. In going to war, there must exist the reasonable expectation of successfully obtaining peace and reconciliation between the warring parties. If going to war will only lead to severe suffering and destruction without a fairly high probability of achieving a just peace, then the outcome is clearly disproportionate to the violent means used.

Jus in Bello   Justice in the Midst of War

Proportionality. The suffering and devastation of war always threaten to outweigh whatever benefits may result. When that happens, force has become arbitrary in yet another way. The standard of proportionality declares that the weapons, tactics, and strategy of warfare must be morally efficient, so to speak. In the interests of achieving a just peace, there must be no "waste," human or otherwise.

Discrimination or Noncombatant Immunity. Deliberately and directly assaulting innocent people, or threatening so to assault them, is taken in just war thinking to be something intrinsically wrong, or "wrong-in-itself." That is, for example, why hostage-taking is prohibited by the tradition. The means of warfare, thus, must discriminate between combatants and noncombatants, between those who pose a mortal threat and those who do not. Even combatants who happen to be disarmed, or otherwise "outside of combat," must also be treated with special consideration.

Just War Standards in the Modern World

So long as Christianity was the official religion and in a dominant political position, force was used not only for secular purposes, but also to advance the Christian cause. In that respect, just war doctrine was explicitly "Christian." But with the disintegration of the medieval establishment and the emergence in the modern period of a sharper separation between civil and ecclesiastical spheres, just war doctrine gradually became secularized, and the role of Christian churches in war-making declined.

That was not a complete break with tradition. Just war thinking had always drawn from "pagan philosophy," and was consistently understood, even during the Middle Ages, as part of "natural law"—knowable through human reason—rather than "revealed law"—knowable through sacred scripture or other divine inspiration. Human beings everywhere, Christian or no, were taken to be capable of understanding that force must be restrained.

The modern age has strengthened that conviction. Hugo Grotius, one of the fathers of modern just war thinking, declared that the restraints have validity "even if we should concede . . . there is no God." Detached from particular religious identity, just war standards could now more easily become a common basis for managing conflict among states with diverse religious and cultural perspectives.

It can be argued, in fact, that the modern international law of war, as expressed in the Hague Regulations of 1899 and 1907 and later in the United Nations Charter, as well as in the Geneva Conventions of 1949 and the Protocols of 1977, codifies and elaborates aspects of just war standards.

For example, Article 2(4) of the UN Charter, which prohibits being the first to initiate a threat of force against another state, enshrined the idea that force must be defensive, in keeping with modern just war doctrine. Along the same lines, Article 51 acknowledges the inherent right of national self-defense as a just cause for using force. Chapter VII identifies the Security Council as the ultimate legitimate authority for determining when force may be employed among states. Articles 41 and 42 express the standard of last resort. They imply that force may be authorized only after other less violent measures have been tried.

As the instruments of "humanitarian law," the Geneva Conventions and Protocols lay down limits of force *in bello,* by prescribing and elaborating the standards of discrimination and proportionality. For example, Article 48 of the First Geneva Protocol requires that military operations respect the distinctions "between the civilian population and combatants and between civilian objects and military objectives." Article 50.5 (b) provides that attacks causing indirect and unintentional injury to civilians "must not be excessive in relation to the concrete and direct military advantage anticipated."

THE SYMPOSIUM DISCUSSION

The discussion at the March 1992 symposium gave evidence that the just war tradition is, in certain circles, still vital and relevant to the moral assessment of war. Several Christian participants were joined by some Jews and Muslims in defending the pertinence of just war standards for deciding when, where, and how force should be used in resolving present-day conflicts. Even though they might not all apply the standards to the same effect in a case like the Gulf War, those favoring the tradition found it hard to imagine forsaking or disregarding these time-honored and now internationally sanctioned restraints.

That Jews and Muslims, out of their own traditions, found points of contact with just war standards lent support to the idea that the standards are not peculiarly Christian. For Jews, the Talmud permits force only when it is duly authorized, justified, and otherwise limited by considerations of discrimination, proportionality, and so forth. The Qur'an and the traditions of interpretation impose restrictions on force similar to just war standards. In Islamic thought, questions of legitimate authority and just cause have been especially important, as have limits on the conduct of war.

There may be differences of emphasis among the three religions over interpreting and applying the standards. It was suggested, for example, that the Jewish tradition has perhaps been more emphatic about restricting environmental destruction in wartime than has the conventional understanding. Islam has required that in wartime Muslims exercise greater restraint toward fellow Muslims, whether combatants or noncombatants, than toward non-Muslims. These and other variations should, no doubt, be the subject of continuing conversation among the three faiths. Still, the common reference points provide a good reason to keep talking.

Because just war thinking is something of a compromise for many Christians, and therefore sits rather uneasily in the tradition, doubts and reservations about it abound. Throughout the centuries, pacifists have tended to believe that such thinking surrenders the essential elements of the faith, while at the other extreme crusaders have often held that just war standards unduly inhibit the cause of righteousness.

The reservations coming from the pacifist side were particularly evident in the symposium, though the pacifists were joined in their skepticism by nonpacifists from all three of the religious groups. In reference to the Gulf War, several participants expressed the fear that despite its promise of restraining and containing force, just war doctrine actually became little more than a pretext and a cover for arbitrary violence. That is the result of the vagueness and indeterminacy of the standards, of the fact that they can so easily be twisted and turned to yield conflicting verdicts in a given case. Concern was also expressed that accepting and concentrating on just war standards encourages people to condone the use of force prematurely, rather than to seek peaceful alternatives and to understand that force often intensifies rather than reduces conflict.

Even those participants inclined to defend allied action in the Gulf on just war grounds felt some of the force of these skeptical comments. Whether the level of military and civilian casualties was ultimately "proportional" to the objectives of the Gulf War, whether more should have been done to discriminate between military and civilian targets in the bombing campaign, were widely acknowledged as abiding perplexities, no matter what final judgment was made about them.

One crucial and overarching challenge to the just war tradition was posed, but not resolved. Is the just war framework, after all, too legalistic, too oversubtle to be morally acceptable? Is it possible that just war standards, focusing as they do on the rights and wrongs of a particular conflict, actually constrict understanding by obscuring broader and more subtle aspects and implications of a situation? Might it, in a given instance, be right to use force, but not good to do it?

By raising and exploring such problems as this, the March symposium proved a stimulating and constructive continuation of the interfaith dialogue begun during the Gulf War. The United States Institute of Peace hopes that this report on the symposium will encourage further reflection and debate among those who try to think morally and religiously about using force.

RELIGIOUS PERSPECTIVES ON WAR

THE AGENDA FOR DISCUSSION

On March 19, 1992, a group of twenty-four thinkers, writers, and scholars met in Washington, D.C., to discuss religious attitudes toward the use of force in international relations. Representing a broad diversity of opinion within the Christian, Jewish, and Muslim faiths, the two dozen participants were keenly aware that their topic had not only enduring theological importance but also profound contemporary relevance. The recent Gulf War, a war in which religion, religious leaders, and religious doctrines had played an influential role, animated and informed much of the day's debate. At the same time, however, the participants were mindful of the weight of both secular and religious history and conscious of the shadow of the future, a future in which they hoped religious faith and leadership might help restrain the violence that nations have so often employed to advance or defend their secular interests.

The day-long symposium, sponsored by the United States Institute of Peace, was structured around five formal papers, with one formal response to each paper, and then general discussion. Three of the papers were prepared by Christians, one of whom presented the just war perspective, another a point of view on "just peace" (explained below), and the third a pacifist perspective. The fourth and fifth papers presented a Jewish and a Muslim point of view, respectively.

This report broadly follows the course of the day's debate. First, it presents arguments for and against the just war doctrine, especially the use of that doctrine during the war in the Gulf. (It should be noted that when they spoke of the "war," the participants tended to mean the allied military action rather than the Iraqi invasion of Kuwait.) Then it moves on to examine just war criteria in light of the Judaic and Islamic traditions, discovering in them both resonances with and differences from the Christian perspective. A number of suggestions as to how to improve and refine just war criteria—especially so that they reflect recent changes in the nature of modern warfare and societies—are advanced and discussed by members of all three faiths. Next, the report examines two Christian schools of thought—just peace theory and pacifism—that regard just war doctrine with profound suspicion and offer alternative approaches to the regulation and use of violence. The report concludes with a discussion of a number of other issues that arose during the symposium, issues such as the popular appetite for violence and fundamental principles of justice and goodness.

Throughout this report, as throughout the symposium itself, the value of interfaith discussion is strikingly evident, with members of each faith finding themselves sometimes supported, sometimes challenged, and always enlightened by the views of their fellow participants.

THE UTILITY OF JUST WAR CRITERIA:
A CHRISTIAN PERSPECTIVE

Father John Langan, a Jesuit and professor of Christian ethics at Georgetown University, launched the discussion with a paper that asked bluntly, "Was the Gulf War a Good Thing?" Testing the Gulf War against the just war criteria, Langan concluded that the allied response to Iraq's invasion of Kuwait was "imperfectly just," a conclusion shared by many other scholars, religious figures, and policymakers who have defended the allied action as satisfying just war criteria. At the same time, however, Langan recognized that for many other people, equally serious and well-intentioned, the war was terrible, "a catastrophe for humanity and for the peoples of the Middle East, and . . . a moral disgrace for the United States." This critical attitude is shared by many religious leaders, including Pope John Paul II.

Langan came to his own conclusion by reasoning that the U.S.-led coalition had a just cause—the repelling and reversing of aggression—as well as legitimate authority, right intention, and reasonable hope of success. He was less sure that the test of "last resort" had been met, but he generally held that the war passed the *jus ad bellum* criteria.

On the other hand, the actual conduct of the war raised four questions that were morally troubling to Langan. The first question relates to the coalition's strategy in the air war, which put more civilian lives at risk than was required by military necessity or by the coalition's political objectives of forcing Iraq's withdrawal from Kuwait and preventing future Iraqi aggression. Particularly problematic was the destruction of the Iraqi electrical system, which was critical for water filtration and purification and in turn essential for sustaining human life in an industrializing society. This destruction had a devastating impact on infants and young children. Although it was unlikely that this was the intention of the coalition's leadership, "a considerable problem remains about protecting civilians and respecting noncombatant immunity in a war zone." This recognition may necessitate a reevaluation of the lists of acceptable and of unacceptable military targets so that they better reflect new levels of social inter-connectedness between military and civilian spheres, as well as innovations in military technology and strategy.

Langan's second and third questions about the conduct of the war concern proportionality—he concluded that the air war probably inflicted excessive casualties, and discrimination—he saw problems with the attack on Iraqi troops on the road from Kuwait back to Basra, and concluded that "fuller measures should have been taken to ensure that more of the fleeing Iraqi troops would be given an opportunity to surrender." Langan's fourth question is whether hostilities were terminated prematurely. He reasoned that "the rush to conclude hostilities after the coalition's decisive victory in the ground war constituted both a decision for restricted change in the Middle East . . . and a decision to forego significant benefits of victory."

In summary, Langan does not give a simple verdict of "just" or "unjust" to the Gulf War, though his assessment does fit within the just war tradition. In that respect Langan differs, as he pointed out, from a number of Gulf War opponents. "It seems clear to me," he said, "that many of the reservations and criticisms that opponents of the war wanted to raise were not of the sort that could be fitted into the legal and casuistic framework of just war theory." Critics may be shifting the argument from one that is primarily moral and centers around notions of right and wrong, characteristic of true just war determinations, to a broader discussion focusing on questions of good and evil. Those attacking both the just war criteria and the justness of the Gulf War seem to be moving beyond the "fairly well-defined, state-centered, somewhat legalistic criteria of just war theories toward a much wider range of what are thought of as morally relevant considerations."

Realizing that traditional just war theory cannot handle the breadth of this debate, Langan added that many critics of the war, including some critics close to the Vatican, have become convinced that the theory is no longer adequate and that modern warfare can no longer be morally justified:

> Just war theory [said Langan] seems to many of these people as being not good enough, not concerned enough about the harms and evils that inescapably abound in the combination of discipline and chaos that is

found in all wars. The evils that are inherent in warfare and the moral
failures found in governments and social systems combine, in the eyes of
these critics, with the particular evils of this war to ensure that both this
war and any future war will have numerous defects and will fail to comply
with the principle of integrity for actions. War is no longer, in this view, to
be judged to be a recurring and occasionally justifiable evil, which is the
evaluation offered by just war theory.

One source of this unease with the just war tradition, as well as with the
Gulf War, is the observation that dramatic social and political changes
occurred in the former Soviet Union and Eastern Europe largely without
bloodshed. Frequently, the critics are also motivated by a desire for
comprehensive justice, which in turn is shaped by traditions and ideologies
that harbor profound ambivalence about the system of nation-states. The
just war tradition, on the other hand, takes the existence and legitimacy of
nation-states for granted.

Although sensitive to the position articulated by these critics, Langan
believes that the theory continues to provide a valuable set of distinctions and questions for assessing what are inherently very negative
actions and that the theory continues to be helpful "for articulating
moral judgments in adversarial situations." The critics disregard the utility and helpful discipline provided by the theory by opening the discussion to such an array of complex considerations.

Alan Geyer, professor of political ethics at Wesley Theological Seminary, responded to Langan. He stated that he wanted the churches to
preserve the just war tradition, while recognizing that it only poses some
of the significant moral questions about war and peace. "The positive
imperatives of peacemaking and of a just peace, some of which may be
implicit in the just war tradition, call for a much more profound and
comprehensive theological ethic."

The brunt of Geyer's critique focused on Langan's application of just
war theory to the Gulf War, suggesting that a more complex and subtle
interpretation of the just war criteria is needed. In response to Langan's
assertion that the Gulf War met the conditions of just cause, Geyer
argued that his own "ethical methodology seeks to lift up the moral
burdens of history, which typically and in the Gulf case emphatically,
make the claim of just cause . . . morally ambiguous." He contended that

Langan's disregard of U.S. and imperial history in the Middle East, oil interests, and prior Western involvement with Iraq leaves a very one-dimensional, nonhistoric view of just cause.

Geyer further argued that "American disdain" for any negotiated settlement dishonored the standard of last resort and that the standard of legitimate authority posed serious questions in the case of the Gulf War. The overall consequences of the war also raised doubts about whether the criterion of success was fully satisfied.

The positions of Langan and Geyer were closer on *jus in bello* issues, particularly in relation to the destruction of Iraq's infrastructure and the consequences of this devastation for civilians. Geyer asserted that the problem with the just war tradition's "preoccupation with intention to the discounting of consequences, is not only the destructiveness of modern weapons, but now the intermeshing of modern military activities with virtually all other economic and technological systems in a society's infrastructure." As a consequence, almost any system can be legitimately considered a military target, and yet its destruction can entail immense nonmilitary human costs. Proportionality must not only measure military casualties, but also the civilian, environmental, economic, and political costs of war.

Other critiques of Langan's position and of just war theory were more extensive. Jay Lintner, director of the Washington office of the Office for Church in Society of the United Church of Christ, asserted that the just war theory is too often used to justify war, and this was particularly true in the Gulf War. Although a set of moral guidelines elaborated by Christian theologians was used by political leaders to justify the Gulf War, a very large number of religious institutions in this country were opposed to the war. These churches did not oppose intervention, but they did oppose the use of military force. While the original intention of just war theory may have been to impose religiously motivated restraint on the initiation and conduct of war, we have now reached the place where the theory is frequently misused and we should ask, "How can we develop restraints upon the use of just war theory itself?"

One way to avoid misuse would be to develop additional restraints from outside the self-contained just war theory, asking whether war serves the cause of justice and whether alternatives to war have been pursued with sufficient vigor. Lintner went on to assert that one source of the corruption of the just war position is that from the beginning the just war theory was a gift of the church to the king. Lintner's preference would be to approach these issues from an understanding of what God is about in history, and more particularly to seek that understanding from the point of view of the oppressed or from the perspective of those at the bottom, as opposed to trying to serve the purposes of the "king."

Others picked up on the theme that just war theory has not been effective in constraining the use of force, arguing that the theory has been misused by those with decision-making power. Robert Johansen, professor of government and peace studies at the University of Notre Dame, asserted that use of the just war theory, contrary to Christian doctrine, may legitimize the use of force and promote a crusading spirit in which triumphalism prevails. He quoted Father Bryan Hehir, the influential social ethicist, as stating that while the Gulf War was just, it was nevertheless unwise. Johansen asked whether just war criteria are useful if they condone war more easily than do criteria for wisdom. Is Christian doctrine less restrictive than wisdom?

Johansen contended that just war theory is out of date in at least four respects. The first and principal problem is that just war theory is very difficult to apply impartially. Not infrequently one can find both sides to a dispute defending their own use of force on the basis of just war criteria. Second, just war theory is outdated because the UN Charter provides a greater constraint on the use of force than just war thinking does. The charter places strong emphasis on collective decision making and on minimizing violence during the conduct of war in enforcement measures taken under Chapter VII. That chapter also imposes very severe limits on the unilateral use of force. A third problem is that just war theory reflects a very unsophisticated attitude, both psychologically and politically, toward what causes war. Moreover, it only looks at a very short segment of history in considering just cause. Finally, just war practitioners usually do not take seriously enough alternative means available for handling security questions and conflict resolution.

> If the idea of using war as a last resort is to mean anything at all [argued Johansen], it must mean that there is a sincere effort prior to the occasion for war to try to put into place the alternative mechanisms for dispute

resolution that are available. . . . Just war thinking has legitimized the belief that we don't need to build up the institutions of peace because we will have as our last resort the use of force.

There may have been no way other than war to stop Hitler after Munich, but if diplomacy had been more effective a couple of decades earlier, then it might have been possible to prevent Hitler even from coming to power.

Other participants, who advocated the just war position, objected to what they considered the failure of these commentators to appreciate the positive contribution that just war theory has made and continues to make to public policy debate. William O'Brien, professor of government at Georgetown University, pointed out that modern just war doctrine did not gain influence until the late 1950s and early 1960s, largely through the contributions of Paul Ramsey, the Protestant moral theologian. In the thirty years since the modern formulation of just war thought, there has arisen a consciousness of moral issues in military affairs that did not previously exist. Admittedly, just war thinking does not address important issues relating to peacemaking. But "no matter how much we work on peacemaking, there are going to be some occasions for use of armed force, and somebody should be around to caution the people who are using it on what some of the guidelines should be for that use."

It was also argued that the abuse of just war theory is in part attributable to its importance and the impact it has had on public discourse. Just war theory had a considerable and impressive influence on policy debates that led up to the Gulf War. Specialists on just war have lectured at war colleges and to military decision makers in other settings. Many articles have been written, much curiosity has been aroused, and considerable media attention has been given to just war. And this exposure influenced the day-to-day military briefings about such things as protection of civilian life. This much success is bound to be accompanied by some abuse, but the success should not be neglected or belittled. What is called for are efforts to ensure that just war theory is not exploited or manipulated for illegitimate purposes.

The congressional debate on the Gulf War was cited by Rabbi David Saperstein, director of the Religious Action Center of Reform Judaism, as a moving and impressive instance of just war criteria being applied in a discussion of whether or not to declare war. However, although the quality of the congressional deliberations on just cause was high, that debate unfortunately did not consider questions regarding how the war should be conducted, apart from the question of the protection of civilians. Future utilization of just war theory in public and congressional debate ought to include just war conduct also. Despite its shortcomings, that debate contrasted dramatically with the total absence of such debate at the time of the U.S. military actions in Panama and Grenada. Similar congressional discussions before those cases might have altered the course of history.

Another participant, Chuck Fager, a Quaker, pacifist, and author, was not so favorably impressed by the interest policymakers demonstrated in just war criteria during the period preceding the Gulf War. He argued that the use of just war criteria merely provided a rationale before the war and a rationalization after the war was concluded, rather than influencing or altering in any way wartime decision making. Moreover, Fager perceived an avoidance or even a suppression of reflection on the costs of the war, both to the victims of the war and to our society. An example of this is the analyst at the Census Bureau who reportedly almost lost her job because she provided an estimate of Iraqi civilian casualties. A responsible use of just war theory requires full disclosure of data and careful, open reflection.

Another illustration of what Fager considered the misuse of the theory was the series of shifting reasons the administration gave for the war, in hopes of finding one that would strike a responsive chord with the public. This raised doubts about what the real causes were and whether the cause was sufficiently compelling to justify going to war.

Concern was also expressed about the way the coalition forces conducted the war. However much planners and policymakers declared their intentions to restrict the bombing, one critic argued that in practice much of it was indiscriminate. While just war criteria may affect planning, the war does not meet just war criteria if conduct is inconsistent with the criteria. Precisely when the cause seems unquestionably just, as it did to the U.S. administration in the case of the Gulf War, extra vigilance is required to make sure that force is used with due restraint.

Several participants criticized the implicit encouragement given to the

Iraqi Kurds and Shiites to rebel at the end of the war, encouragement that created a secondary war within a war. This U.S. encouragement was thought to be quite unjustified, since there was never any intention to provide American or coalition support for the insurrections once they began. In the end, the Kurds and Shiites suffered terrible punishment at the hands of Saddam Hussein, which subsequently provoked the creation of "security zones" to provide some protection offered by the United Nations and the coalition.

The fact that just war theory may provide legitimation of war on religious grounds could contribute to greater intransigence and increased bloodshed. Moreover, both sides of the conflict may conclude that they are conducting a religiously legitimated just war. Mumtaz Ahmad, professor of political science at Hampton University, argued: "If you feel that you are fighting for a just cause or for a moral cause or for the sake of God and develop a highly exaggerated sense of moral self-righteousness, then you tend to fight to the finish." The invocation of religious justification may stop the powers in conflict from sitting down and negotiating a peace settlement. The Iranian leader Ayatollah Khomeini continued to fight against Iraq for almost nine years because he was convinced he was fighting for God.

THE JEWISH TRADITION

David Novak, professor of Judaic studies at the University of Virginia, argued that although the just war theory has Christian origins and is generally thought to be a Christian doctrine, the just war criteria have firm roots in Jewish thought and scriptures. The categories traditionally subsumed under "just war" all have precedents in the Jewish tradition. However, formulating moral principles regarding war has been more difficult for Jews than for Christians and Muslims, because until very recently Jews commanded no armies and had no political power. As a consequence, Christian and Muslim ethicists have much to contribute to Jewish thinkers on the subject of just war. Nevertheless, there have been discussions throughout Jewish history of what can be termed just war theory. Moreover, it should be noted that while Jews do control armies and political power in Israel, there is still intense debate within Israel about the extent to which the Judaic tradition should inform or govern the decisions of state.

In addition to containing just war principles, this tradition also warns about the dangers of misusing religious authority in making war. The Bible relates instances in which court prophets of Israel pandered to kings by sanctioning their war-making, and in turn these prophets contributed to the erroneous belief that the voice of the king was the voice of God.

Novak also cautioned that from a Jewish perspective, as from the Christian perspective, there should be no triumphalism in war. "Any war involves mistakes. It involves deaths. It involves suffering." Although the Gulf War was justified, both in terms of its protection of Israel and its reversal of the Iraqi invasion of Kuwait, that war, like all wars, involved a choice between the lesser of two evils.

> In the Bible [Novak pointed out], even warriors returning from successful battle were considered unclean and required atoning purification (Num. 31:19-24). Even King David, who fought justified wars, could not build the Temple because God told him "you are a warrior who has shed blood" (1 Chronicles 28:3). The ultimate messianic vision is of the time when "they

will learn warfare no more" (Isaiah 2:4; Micah 4:3). Nevertheless, in the premessianic time, war must be waged under certain circumstances. . . . Peace at any price is not *shalom.* Not all war is justified, but not all war is unjustified either. To know the difference is wisdom. "Trust (*emet*) and just peace (*mishpat shalom*) shall you judge in your gates" (Zech. 8:16). Peace is only possible when bound together with truth and justice. Civilization itself depends on all three (Mishnah: Avot 1.18).

Taking each of the just war criteria in turn, Novak demonstrated its scriptural or Talmudic base. In discussing just cause he pointed out that the Bible endorses peace as the desired state of international relations and war as the undesired exception. Self-defense is justified, but only when there is no alternative. As the Talmud puts it: "When it is certain he is coming to kill you, kill him first" (Sanhedrin 72a). There is also biblical basis for coming to the aid of a victim of aggression, for example in the biblical command that "you not stand idly by the blood of your brother" (Lev. 19:16).

Novak argued that the utility of the just cause criteria as a basis of moral discrimination can be seen in the difference in outcome when they are applied to the Vietnam and the Gulf wars. The Vietnam War was not a legitimate use of force because "it could not be ascertained which side was the aggressor and which side the victim of aggression. In cases where this cannot be ascertained, where it is essentially unclear 'who is pursuing whom,' the ancient rabbis ruled for nonintervention (Yerushalmi Shabbat 14.4/14d)."

An important distinction is made in the Judaic literature between optional war and mandated war. If a war is one of immediate self-defense, then it is mandated and authority to wage it is considered self-evident. For any other kind of war, sanction for making war must be based on careful consideration of the context and cause. The twelfth-century scholar Rabbi Moses Maimonides ruled that the reason for waging an optional war had to be a moral one. The object of attack has to have been in violation of universal moral law before a nation can have proper religious authority to wage war.

In addition to mandated and optional wars, a third category of war is alluded to in the rabbinic sources. Called *milhemet hovah* (best translated as "war of conquest"), this category of holy war is, however, limited by the Talmud to the wars the Israelites waged against the Canaanites in the days of Joshua.

The Jewish literature provides abundant justification for the criterion that in any use of force good must outweigh evil in the final outcome. In the deuteronomic injunction "Justice, justice you shall pursue" (Deut. 16:20), we see the urging of justice as the final outcome. The Biblical prohibition against a scorched-earth policy is similarly reasoned and is specifically cited in Deut. 20:19-20. "In Jewish tradition this passage was generalized into a prohibition of 'wanton destruction' (Kiddushin 32a)." By Novak's reckoning, this principle clearly differentiated the conduct of the Gulf War by the coalition forces and by Saddam Hussein, with the former "avoiding unnecessary damage to both civilian lives and to the environment" and the latter engaging in wholesale ecological destruction merely for the sake of destructiveness.

The principle of war as a last resort is rooted in the biblical injunction, "When you approach a town to attack it, you shall offer it terms of peace" (Deut. 20:10). Peace is the first concern, and war should be the last. Two additional texts (Deut. 2:26 and Judges 11:12) show that peace is always to be pursued before war. Novak argued that these injunctions were heeded in the UN coalition's approach to the Gulf War, but unfortunately all efforts to negotiate peace were arrogantly rejected by Saddam Hussein. Novak cited several biblical passages to demonstrate that restraints on the use of force are rooted in the Jewish scriptures as well.

Although the major thrust of Novak's presentation was to demonstrate the parallels between a Christian-based and a Jewish-based just war theory, Rabbi Saperstein noted some areas in which Jewish just war theory and Christian attitudes toward war differ. He also noted in passing that Jewish and Islamic attitudes are somewhat more similar than either is to Christian thinking.

Saperstein pointed out that for Christians the notion of right authority is one of the least defined, most amorphous, of the criteria. In the Jewish tradition, because it is a tradition of laws, there is greater clarity on this point. Most Jewish interpreters believe that in the case of a preemptive war or an offensive war—that is, one not fought strictly in self-defense— the supreme council of Jews, the Sanhedrin, had to be involved in making the decision. Such a decision could not be left to the executive alone. The Sanhedrin was part representative of the people, part legislative body, part judicial body, and part protector of society's moral norms. Its closest American equivalent is the Congress. Hence, the kind of congressional debate that took place regarding participation in the Gulf War is exactly the kind of debate that Jewish tradition envisions.

Second, Saperstein, unlike Novak, was unable to find a Jewish parallel for the concept of last resort. What is required is a good faith effort to avoid war, but beyond that the prescriptions are very limited. "It seems to me that the Christian tradition, being much more of a literal last resort tradition, can make a far more powerful argument about the need to have exhausted sanctions and all other alternatives than the Jewish tradition requires."

A third difference lies in the concept of proportionality. Some minor themes in the Jewish tradition allude to proportionality, but the Jewish tradition is principally concerned with categories where force is permissible and categories where it is impermissible. For instance, it is not permissible to attack innocent civilians or to cut down fruit-bearing trees. But there is no discussion of how many combatants can be killed in battle. "Where military targets are justifiable targets, there is no limitation on the amount of force that could be used to pursue whatever the objective of war is. And in those areas that are exempt from force, you should not do it, period, if it is at all avoidable."

Finally, Saperstein pointed out that the Christian tradition does not share what is in Jewish law a major concern, namely, a concern for the environment. The biblical prohibition against cutting down fruit-bearing trees was later extended by Jewish scholars to anything that produces food or fruit, to storehouses of food, to anything that is used for normal civilian life. The underlying theory seems to be that "just means" requires ensuring that the normalcy of civilian life "be allowed to renew itself after the war and destruction of the civilian infrastructure would be frowned upon." Applying this to Iraq's war-making, much of what Iraq did—including the targeting of civilians, the destruction of the infrastructure of civilian life in Kuwait, the gratuitous dumping of oil into the sea, and the burning of wells during the retreat—collectively constitutes a classic example of behavior that would violate the Jewish tradition. Similarly, the intentional targeting by the allies of the infrastructure of Iraqi civilian life constitutes a violation. According to Jewish law, "there is an absolute and specific prohibition" of such targeting of civilian infrastructure. Some of the Christian debates over the legitimacy of these actions are clearly and unequivocally resolved by Jewish interpretation.

An issue for all religious traditions, and particularly for the Jewish tradition, is the question of how to use ancient texts to develop contemporary moral law. What interpretative canons should be used? Yehudah Mirsky of the Washington Institute for Near East Policy stated: "Anyone employing halachic tradition in order to arrive at an understanding of just war must ascertain their moral and methodological canons of decision making and interpretation." Beyond that, they must of necessity grapple with the central question of Jewish law in modern times, namely, what is the proper source of authority for the law?

Mirsky pointed out that Jews have a particular perspective on nonreligious sources of authority as well. The charter of the United Nations had been mentioned earlier in the discussion as a basis for formulating contemporary moral codes. But, said Mirsky, given the historically unfair treatment of Israel by the United Nations, Israelis and other Jews are unlikely to look to the United Nations as a source of moral authority. "As a Jew who has a very genuine commitment to the survival of the State of Israel, I could be expected to hold a somewhat jaundiced view of the United Nations."

The respondent to Novak's paper, Professor Gershon Greenberg from American University, differed with Novak's perspective in several respects. While Novak contended that there should be a particular Judaic response drawn from Jewish tradition, which in turn lends itself to such universal values as just cause, last resort, and proportionality, Greenberg asserted that from his perspective the Gulf War was "particularly Jewish." Although Israel's isolation during the 1967 war was certainly not repeated here, "The Gulf War still brought forth, evoked once again, the reality of the Holocaust, as the '67 war did." Israel could have been destroyed. The Jewish baseline was extinction, not life. And in this instance, "Jews were manacled from defending themselves not by lack of arms this time, but by world and American needs." The recollection of the Holocaust trauma and the resonance back to World War II were very real.

Greenberg also argued that the Gulf War was particularly Jewish because Saddam Hussein managed to convince some portions of the world that the real occupiers were not the Iraqis but Jews and Israel. Saddam Hussein renewed the ancient theme that there was somebody else who could be blamed, and they were the Jews.

According to Greenberg, World War II and the Holocaust shattered the universal grounding of morality:

> In the ontology left by the Holocaust [said Greenberg], universal morality exploded into smithereens. . . . As far as Jewry is concerned, the categorical moral imperative of [the eighteenth-century German philosopher] Immanuel Kant has been shattered by the self-defined rationale for murder of Adolf Eichmann [the Nazi who oversaw the implementation of the Holocaust in World War II]. . . . The Judaic response to the war should have enunciated this particularity.

In response to the Gulf War there should have been an assertive Jewish voice raised, and it should have been raised to promote Jewish survival. The universalistic concerns about Iraqi aggression and the assessment of whether the military response to that was just or not just should have been secondary concerns from the perspective of Judaism.

Hence the Gulf War raised questions for Jews of absolute or even mythic justice, which tragically is the legacy of the Jews after World War II. After World War II the survival of Judaism and of Jewry is the highest value, and that is the lens through which Jews must of necessity view the Gulf War and any other war in which their survival is at stake.

A somewhat different position on Jewish survival was expressed by Mirsky. "The survival of Jewry in its own right and on its own terms is in many ways the central value after the Holocaust. But at a certain point the survival of Jewry has to be given a certain content." The deeper meaning may be that the right of Jewish survival "functions almost as a metasymbol [a deep metaphor] of the right of human beings to survive," much in the way that in the Lurianic Kabbalah the exile of Israel is taken as a metasymbol of God's exile from the world or, in some ultimate sense, God's exile from Himself.

Mirsky went on to point out two different levels of discourse possible in relation to the Gulf War, one of which might be characterized as rabbinic and the other as prophetic. "The prophetic critique of power, authority, and sovereignty is in a deep sense timeless, standing over and above historical time and in judgment of historical time. The rabbinic perspective is more timely and time-bound, operating within an unredeemed world." The classical rabbinic effort is to maintain a dialectical relationship between prophetic time and rabbinic time, just as the Sabbath exists in dialectical relationship with the rest of the week. The rabbinic tradition exists in the tension between historical time, focusing on sheer Jewish survival, and prophetic time, which involves the transfiguration of human time by the divine.

THE ISLAMIC TRADITION

M. M. Ali of the University of the District of Columbia provided an Islamic perspective. He noted that the Islamic state is allowed to go to war against those who commit aggression against it. "The Qur'an is very clear on the subject: 'And fight in the way of Allah those who fight you, but commit no aggression, for Allah does not love aggression.'" The noted Muslim theologian Ibn Taymiyah explains that the initiation of attacks on others is only justified when the practice of Islam is being obstructed. The much misunderstood and much misinterpreted *jihad* is prescribed only in cases when oppression must be eliminated, human life protected, and Islamic principles upheld.

Ali pointed out that since the spiritual orientation of the principal executors of the Gulf War was not Islamic and since Islamic prescriptions relating to the initiation and conduct of war all relate to Muslim states, it is not possible to apply these prescriptions to the Gulf War. That Muslims did not view the war from a religious perspective was evident from the total unresponsiveness of Muslims to Saddam Hussein's call for a *jihad.*

It is difficult to assess whether the Gulf War was a just war because in some sense the war is still continuing. Moreover, not all the data are yet available. Ali contended that vital information, including the number of civilian casualties, has been unavailable, even suppressed. Expressing an aversion to military conflicts, he observed: "When Kuwait gets attacked, I get hurt. When Iraq gets attacked, I get hurt."

In employing the Christian just war criteria, Ali asked that we recognize that the theory is curiously apolitical and insufficiently historical. He quoted from James Graff's article, "The Gulf War: Just or Obscene?" (in Bha Abu-laban and Ibrahim Aladin, eds., *Beyond the Gulf War* [Edmonton, Vancouver: MRF Publications, 1991]), in objecting to "the tendency of the theory to treat collectivities as if they were individuals" and in the process to ignore the sufferings of helpless citizens of the aggressor state. Graff asked:

> Suppose that there was no entrapment, no provocation by . . . the Kuwaiti regime, no special U.S. interest in exploiting the crisis to secure leverage . . . and to preserve a profitable arrangement with the Gulf regimes. Suppose, in short, that everything which skews the application of just war theory was not true. Would the war have been justified?

Ali doubted that the last resort provisions of the criteria were satisfied, and he wondered if all peaceful avenues were exhausted and if sanctions were given sufficient time to work. He also had difficulty finding a straightforward answer to the standard of right authority. In addition, he found the right intention criterion to be an immeasurable factor. "There are hidden agendas within agendas. What is publicly professed may not always reflect the whole truth. Truth unfortunately continues to be the first casualty in war." In terms of proportionality he asked whether it is proportional when 100,000 soldiers were killed on the ground in 100 hours—a rate of 1,000 deaths per hour. After reviewing the attacks that severely damaged civilian areas and civilian infrastructures, he doubted that the proportionality criterion was satisfied.

In summary, Ali stated: "The spirit in which the just war theory has been formulated is without any doubt noble. The issue is how best to protect it from being used to legitimize and justify wars of all kinds."

The respondent, Professor John Kelsay of the Department of Religion at Florida State University, took exception to Ali's paper in several respects. He expressed disappointment that Ali did not address the justice of the Gulf War (or lack of it) from a specifically Islamic point of view. Contrary to Ali's assertion that the war did not lend itself to analysis from an Islamic perspective, there were many vigorous discussions among Muslims about the war. Varied judgments about the war were offered by Pakistani Islamic activists, for example. The opinions (*fatawa*) issued by jurists in Saudi Arabia and Egypt regarding aspects of the war were vigorously debated in various parts of the Muslim world. Several Islamic jurists in Jordan issued formal opinions about the war.

Kelsay argued that Ali's paper is also incomplete in its presentation of the rich and complex contributions that Islam can make to a discussion of the ethics of war:

> Through their long history [said Kelsay], Muslims have had ample experience in considering the connections between religion, morality, and statecraft. The meaning of defense, the possibility of wars to extend Islamic territory, the nature of treaties, and above all the question of rules for the conduct of war—all these have been discussed by Muslim jurists in connection with particular instances of the use of force.

Kelsay went on to suggest several ways in which the Islamic tradition might be applied to the Gulf War. First, he discussed the distinction between *jihad*, a war fought in accordance with the purposes and limits determined by God, and *harb*, which is every other kind of war. One way for Muslims to discuss the Gulf War would be to argue that it exemplifies the latter type of war; that the motivations of the participants were not Islamically authentic and therefore that it was not surprising that their conduct did not respect Islamic rules of conduct of war. Islam makes the claim that "the best way to limit the occasion and damage of war is to keep *jihad* as the [only] 'truly just war.'"

Another way for Muslims to analyze the Gulf War (and one that Kelsay thought specifically promising) would be to apply the standards that Muslim jurists called *ahkam al-bughat* (literally, "the judgments of the tyrants"), which were particularly developed for wars between Muslims. Applying these standards to the Gulf War, one might conclude that Iraq was the offending party, while the Muslim members of the coalition fought in a just cause. But Kelsay identified the following problems with this simplistic conclusion:

> First, the involvement of non-Muslim forces; second (and more importantly), the *jus in bello* provisions of Islamic law are more strict with respect to wars between Muslims than in other cases. From the perspective of *al-bughat*, the coalition's aerial strategy would have to be evaluated according to this saying of Ali b. Abi Talib, the son-in-law of the Prophet: "Whoever flees [from us] shall not be chased, no [Muslim] prisoner of war shall be killed, no wounded in battle shall be dispatched, no enslavement [of women and children] shall be allowed, and no property [of a Muslim] shall be confiscated."

Providing a third perspective on Islam, Professor Mumtaz Ahmad of the Department of Political Science at Hampton University pointed out that the Islamic tradition is similar to the Jewish tradition in that it is basically a mediated tradition, mediated by jurists as Jewish thought is mediated by rabbis and scholars. Hence, there is no direct access to the text, and to understand Islamic doctrine regarding war one must turn to the writing and pronouncements of jurists.

The classical doctrine of *jihad* and the legal rules and principles regarding war were developed under specific historical conditions in Islamic history, particularly the struggle between the Islamic state under the Abbasids and the Christian West. The jurists were responding to specific historical circumstances and had no intention of developing a comprehensive theory of war. Modern interpreters, recognizing the historical specificity of the classical theory, have sought additional guidance from the Qur'an and the Sunna of the Prophet (the body of Islamic customs and practice based on the Prophet's words and deeds). There is no consensus even among classical jurists; hence, one cannot identify a single classical theory of Islam in relation to war.

Ahmad nevertheless identified four situations under which Islam would justify war. He drew these conclusions based on a reading of classical formulations and a modern interpretation of Islamic theory of war, as articulated by modernists, liberal Muslims, and fundamentalist Muslim thinkers. The first situation in which war is justified "is eliminating oppression and protection of human life, ensuring the free observance of religion; secondly, defending Islamic territories against foreign aggression; thirdly, defending and restoring the rights of those who have been driven from their homes; and, finally, upholding the authority of the Islamic state against armed rebellion, *kharuj*." And it is in this latter respect that Islamic political theory is most fully developed.

In looking for Muslim assessments regarding the Gulf War, Ahmad identified three sources of data, one being the opinions, pronouncements, and decrees issued by the *'ulama;* second, the writings of independent Muslim intellectuals; and third, the statements of Islamic fundamentalist movements. Regarding the statements of the *'ulama*, there is a sharp difference of view expressed by those on the payroll of the allied forces and those who worked for Iraq. Statements of the *'ulama* from Saudi

Arabia and Egypt justified Saudi Arabia's going to war and stated that Saudi Arabia was Islamically justified in seeking help from non-Muslims. This latter justification was supported by the fact that when Prophet Muhammad was militarily weak in Mecca he sought and received help from the Christian king of Ethiopia. However, a gathering of *'ulama* in Baghdad just prior to the beginning of the war concluded that it was a religious obligation, a *jihad*, for Muslims to support Saddam Hussein and fight against the allied forces to protect the integrity of the Islamic community (*ummah*). "So we see that the position taken is not on juristic grounds, but where you stand politically, your political connections, political alliances, as the dominant criterion."

Muslim intellectuals and scholars generally concluded that the Gulf War was a situation of *harb*, a secular war. "Neither the Saudis nor the Iraqis are fighting for the sake of Islam. It is a struggle for secular power and territory. Islam and religion have nothing to do with it." On the other hand, the Islamic fundamentalists, who are basically political activists and not concerned with "doctrinal and theological hair-splitting," argued that the most important issue at stake was the integrity of the *ummah*. "The presence of Iraqi troops in Kuwait is bad, but the presence of half a million American troops [in the heart of Islam] is even worse. If Kuwait has been lost, it has not been lost to non-Muslims. It's still within the Islamic *ummah*. But the victory of the allied forces will have catastrophic consequences for the Islamic world. Today it is Iraq, tomorrow it will be Iran, and the day after tomorrow, it will be Pakistan." That was the basis for fundamentalist opposition to the war.

Based upon this analysis, Ahmad concluded: "No fresh and fundamental juristic and religious rethinking took place within broad Islamic discourse as a result of the Gulf War. The primary concerns were political and the possible political consequences of the war for the Islamic world."

HOW TO REFINE AND IMPROVE
JUST WAR CRITERIA

These discussions of just war theory in the three faith traditions sparked suggestions of how just war criteria might be improved to take into account the complexities of history and morality and the changing nature of modern political, social, and military arrangements.

One major difficulty encountered in applying the just war theory, according to Kelsay, is that it generally lacks "historical thickness." Kelsay has experienced considerable difficulty in building an appropriate historical narrative into just war reasoning, as illustrated by the Gulf War. He said that we could start with a short-term narrative, with the August invasion of Kuwait, and build from there. Or we could talk in terms of a long-term narrative that would show American complicity in building up the Iraqi military machine during the war with Iran:

> I suppose if we wanted to get at the roots of that [Kelsay continued], we would have to start with the fall of the Shah, because that was what created instability between Iran and Iraq. And the rise of the Khomeini regime was what made it seem attractive to shore up Iraq as the foot soldier of Arab and American interests in the Gulf region. On the other hand, if we wanted to push back far enough, we would really have to start in post-World War II with the American installation of the Shah and the development of increasing oppression, a sense of being cut off from historic rights among the Shiite clergy in Iran. If we push back further, we could start from the fall of the caliphate after World War I, which created all kinds of problems. . . . Or maybe we would like to go back to Ottoman imperialism. After all, . . . it was there that the whole pattern of a coalition between Sunni Muslims and Christians running the territory that we call Iraq at the expense of other minorities was started. . . . If we want to talk about historical thickness, where do we start?

Saddam Hussein wanted us to start with Saladin driving out the crusaders, or sometimes he said he wanted us to start with the Abyssinian and

Babylonian empires. Ibn Kaldoun, the great Muslim historian, thought we should start with the creation.

One area in which interfaith dialogue has helped develop a consensus among the participants is that "discrimination" should pertain not just to deaths of people, but also to destruction of the environment and of infrastructure. This is a particularly strong principle within the Jewish tradition, which articulates the injunction that war should not be conducted in a way that prohibits the return to normal civilian life following the end of hostilities. Saperstein argued that the just war criteria should be revised and refined to make it more difficult for the next war to occur, and, "should it come about, being fought in a way that preserves human life, preserves the environment, preserves the infrastructure of normalcy of life better than occurred in the [Gulf War]."

The "in-between targets in the infrastructure" concerned Kelsay as well, particularly those targets that can have a military purpose but primarily have a civilian purpose. To be responsive to the realities of modern warfare, Kelsay urged, just war theory needs to address the problem of indirect and direct targeting. For instance, "if water filtration devices depend on electrical grids, which are important for military mechanisms, when one hits the electrical grid, what is the culpability for the water filtration system?" A strike against the electrical grid can serve a military purpose but can have a disastrous impact on civilian welfare as well.

Langan advocated sharper definition of the principle of proportionality, calling it a "very slippery category." No one can provide a calculus or a satisfactory set of values to equate Kuwaiti independence with "X" many lives. Judgments regarding proportionality are largely impressionistic. Consequently it is very difficult to obtain agreement, particularly across cultures, on what constitutes proportionality. The question of proportionality could be raised about World War II, but in that case one must also consider how many lives would have been lost if there had been no resistance to Hitler. To some extent proportionality can only be judged retrospectively, after the war process has been concluded. Moreover, it is legitimate for an army to conduct a war in such a way as to minimize its own casualties, since war is an adversarial exercise. "So it is possible that the line of disproportionate outcomes is crossed without either side making a culpable decision, . . . given the fact that you are initiating a series of processes, the precise outcome of which you can not control well." And yet some uses of force would still count as disproportionate because they are excessive in relation to the objective achieved.

The appropriate use of the just war theory requires that all the criteria be applied. James Matlack, director of the Washington Office of the American Friends Service Committee, pointed out that in the case of the Gulf War there was a tendency to say that because there was a just cause it was a just war. The provocation was so clear that the other categories were all subsumed under just cause. He went on to ask whether the execution of a war might entail such gross misconduct or such destructiveness that the justice of the cause becomes irrelevant in determining whether the war is just. Matlack contended that given the devastating firepower of modern weapons and the devastation of modern ways of war, such an outcome might be inevitable. What is so worrisome is that analysts frequently neglect the rest of the criteria because just cause is given such prominence. Once a just cause is assumed, then the conduct of the war escapes moral judgment. As a consequence, in the process of refining and clarifying the criteria, balance must be achieved between just cause and the other criteria. By none of the three faith traditions can the end be made to justify the means.

Another issue relating to just cause also needs attention, said Langan. Langan pointed out that just cause is almost exclusively interpreted as relating to the behavior of nation-states rather than of subnational units. The initial attitude toward the Iraqi Kurds on the part of the Bush administration illustrates this misinterpretation of the just cause criterion. In the utilization of the just war criteria, one finds "a pro-state bias of a much stronger sort than I would think is required by the Catholic tradition."

The Islamic tradition can be helpfully used to clarify the meaning of "success," Ahmad pointed out. He explained that from the perspective of Islam, cessation of hostilities per se is not the achievement of peace. "Peace, according to Islam, means not the restoration of status quo ante, that is the reinstallment of the emir of Kuwait, as the moral objective of the peaceful condition, but the absence of oppression, tyranny, and injustice and the achievement of objectives for which the war itself was legitimized." A group called American Muslims United for Peace developed a set of objectives for achieving peace in the Gulf in that Islamic sense. First, they unconditionally condemned the Iraqi invasion of Kuwait. Second, they called for equal attention to the long-term injustices committed against the Palestinians, and they urged implementation of UN Resolution 242 as a basis for settling the Arab-Israeli conflict. The allied coalition was called upon to broker a Middle East peace process and to promote democracy, liberalization, and respect for human rights throughout the region. Their proposals called for democracy in both the modern dictatorships and the medieval dictatorships and monarchies of the region. They identified serious violations of human rights not only in Iraq, but also in Saudi Arabia and elsewhere, and argued that a true peace necessitated political reforms and redistribution of economic resources throughout the region.

The application of just war theory by an important subgroup of the military was highlighted by Matlack. He pointed to the "refusers and resisters variously situated who were called, and for one reason or another faced that choice and felt they could not go." They refused to go because they concluded that the war either did not have a just cause or was not likely to be conducted in a just manner. Matlack called for more effective provision within the military for those struggling with issues of conscientious objection and refusal to wage war.

A frequently repeated theme was the need to modify and refine just war criteria by taking account of new wartime situations. Reference, for instance, was made to discussions among Muslim theorists at the time of the Iran-Iraq war about how to handle chemical weapons within the criterion of proportionality. Iranian moral philosophers and religious leaders asked themselves whether, on the basis of proportionality, Iran was entitled to use chemical weapons in responding to the Iraqi use of chemical weapons. They wondered whether any benefit might justify retaliating with such grotesque weapons.

Professor Walter Wink of Auburn Theological Seminary articulated five points relating to violence reduction upon which he believed pacifists, or people committed to nonviolence, and just war theorists could agree. These five points might provide a basis for some convergence among those who think just war criteria are valuable but insufficiently historical, subtle, or extensive, and those who advocate a nonviolence or pacifist position. The first point is that nonviolence is preferable to violence. Second, the innocent must be protected as much as possible. Third, persons holding both positions would reject any defense of a war motivated solely by such matters as a crusade mentality or personal egocentricity. Fourth, at no point would either group want to suspend morality. And finally, both sides wish to persuade states to reduce the levels of violence in any situation of armed conflict.

Whether convergence is possible on such points depends in large part, Johansen pointed out, on how much peace people think is possible. "For those who think that a lot of peace is possible, they are either going to dismiss just war criteria because they do not need them to find convincing reasons that most wars are unnecessary or they are going to work very hard to try to refine them and improve them to such a point that a careful application of just war criteria will lead to the conclusion that almost no wars are justifiable." Stating that he is one of those who believes that peace is possible, Johansen continued:

> I would use just war criteria myself if I could apply them more sensitively and upgrade them and make them more responsive to what I think are contemporary understandings of political realities so that those who are committed to just war criteria would move closer and closer to the conclusion that we cannot find any wars that are justifiable anymore.

All the faith traditions represented at the workshop bring a presupposition against violence, and they can help each other to develop violence reduction criteria. Regardless of whether a consensus has been reached about whether just war criteria have continued utility, interfaith dialogue can help develop principles for political conduct that "would reduce the likelihood of war and reduce the bloodiness of it when it occurs," argued Johansen.

A JUST PEACE PERSPECTIVE

The "just peace" perspective was presented by Professor Susan Thistlethwaite of Chicago Theological Seminary. The just peace theory was originally proposed many years ago by the Federal Council of Churches and has more recently been developed and advocated by the United Church of Christ, as well as by the United Methodists and others. Just peace theory begins with the notion that the weapons revolution has made just war theory outmoded and necessitates its reformulation. "The revolution in the destructiveness of conventional weapons (to say nothing of nuclear, biological, or poison gas weaponry) is so massive that one cannot fight without an unacceptable amount of loss of innocent life." New occasions teach new duties, and new weapons require new forms of moral reflection.

Professor Thistlethwaite summarized some of the distinctiveness of the just peace position by stating:

> If you think of just war, just peace, and pacifism as a continuum of moral reflection, the theological anthropology that undergirds just peace theory would be more suspicious of the fallenness of the human condition than . . . is present in pacifism, but it is more social than the more individualistic emphasis on human fallenness that you find in just war theory.

She argued that the social phenomenon of war needs to be considered. "It is not, according to just peace theory, inevitable that human beings, while sinful, fallen, and prone to conflict, will inevitably go to war out of that fallenness. How human societies regard war is a product of our social reflection."

While just war theory has focused on common security from violence, just peace represents a mutually supportive relationship between friendship and justice along with common security from violence. A thorough analysis of the causes of the Gulf War would not focus exclusively on Iraq's invasion of Kuwait, but would need to consider the full range of historical factors, including injustices done to Iraq. Not that consideration of these factors would justify Iraq's invading Kuwait, but it would elucidate the issues that need to be addressed if true peace is to be achieved. "The Middle East as a whole will never have a just peace, and will rarely even have the minimal of the absence of overt conflict, until the long-standing injustices in the region are brought to the table and adjudicated." Nor, according to Thistlethwaite, have the issues that precipitated the Gulf War been resolved in a manner that will promote peace.

A second basic principle of just peace is that peace is possible. "A just peace is a basic gift of God and is the force and vision moving human history." Just war theorists, on the other hand, proceed from the assumption that peace, while desirable, is not really possible. "Just peace theory assumes that human self-interest can be activated to find a negotiated settlement and that were more time and energy devoted to the development of sophisticated negotiation, more and more conflicts could be addressed without resort to armed conflict." In contrast to the rather pathetic attempts at diplomacy prior to the outbreak of the Gulf War, she said that one has to intend peace to achieve peace, and "sword rattling and humiliation are not the overtures from which a negotiated settlement is constructed."

A third principle of just peace theory, as articulated by Thistlethwaite, is that "the *meaning* of a just peace and God's activity in human history is understood through the Bible, church history, and the voices of the oppressed and those in the struggle for justice and peace." The victims of war, who are overwhelmingly women, children, and the elderly, provide a more accurate and authentic perspective on war. Their experiences need to be given a central place in any effort to reflect on war. Another silent victim of war is the environment, and we need to recognize that justice and peace have an inseparable relationship to the integrity of creation.

Additional central tenets of just peace theory are (1) that nonviolence is an inadequately explored but authentically Christian response to conflict, and (2) that violence can and must be minimized or even eliminated. Moreover, war can and must be eliminated. There are alternative ways to settle disputes; war is not inevitable.

The mere existence of just war theory raises several troubling points for Thistlethwaite and for other just peace theorists. Given the human capacity for self-deception and rationalization:

> it is inevitable [said Thistlethwaite] that the existence of a set of criteria for considering whether war is just under any circumstance will offer ample opportunities for human beings who wish to wage war to rationalize that their reasons for doing so are just. This is demonstrably the way just war theory has functioned in human history. No war has been just by all the criteria of just war theory during the whole of a conflict; every war has been called a just war by the leaders on both sides of the conflict. It is certainly worth considering then whether the existence of just war theory . . . is itself one of the reasons Western culture has so readily accepted war as one of its social mores.

Just peace theory assumes that war is unjust, rather than asking whether war can be just. It posits that war should be "eliminated from human history, that conflict be negotiated and that violence in all human relationships be minimized by the rule of law." In turn, it is a more difficult theory than just war theory under which to rationalize one's actions as being just.

Suspicion is a key criterion of just peace theory, and any assertion, based upon just war criteria, of war's being justified to protect others must be the subject of suspicion. "Suspicion of self-interest must always be a central factor in assessing why war is deemed an acceptable strategy." Thistlethwaite asserted that this was certainly the case with the Gulf War, since Iraq's invasion of Kuwait was not the only factor that prompted Desert Storm. She contended that domestic political interests were important and possibly the principal determining factors. This prevailing sense of suspicion that characterizes the interpretation of government policies by just peace advocates might be termed a "hermeneutics of suspicion."

Another central principle of just peace theory is that international structures of friendship, justice, and common security from violence are both necessary and possible, and can help eliminate the institution of war. Although the potential effectiveness of the United Nations was not fully realized in the Gulf War, just peace advocates celebrate the renewed role the United Nations is playing in international conflict. The UN Charter is solidly on the side of negotiated settlements and nonmilitary approaches to international crises. Thistlethwaite regretted that negotiations and economic sanctions were not given a sufficient opportunity to affect the outcome of the Gulf crisis.

A final just peace principle is the advocacy of "unexpected initiatives of friendship and reconciliation," which hold the potential for transforming international relationships and restoring community. Behind this principle is the assumption that a business-as-usual approach to international conflict will produce a business-as-usual result. Thistlethwaite contended that the business-as-usual approach adopted in the case of the Gulf by the coalition powers produced a situation in which the Middle East is not significantly better off than it was before the war. Unexpected initiatives require creativity and new approaches. And these unexpected initiatives must not go only the second mile, but the third, the fourth, and the fifth.

"Just war perspectives have aggravated [an] American tendency to think of war as a game where someone wins and someone loses," Thistlethwaite concluded. "Just peace proponents recognize that there is just one game—life. And the game goes on."

Responding to Thistlethwaite's paper, Professor Robert Holmes of the Department at Philosophy of the University of Rochester expressed general concurrence with her argument. He shared Thistlethwaite's concern that assertions of the just cause of the Gulf War tended to disregard the many complex justice issues imbedded in centuries of regional history. "We cannot fully understand the war and U.S. involvement in the region apart from an understanding of the culture, religion, and history of the peoples of the region and [the history of] their domination by outside powers."

Holmes' second area of agreement was that the just war theory has become an impediment to creative new thinking about the moral problem of war. While the theory itself has some merit and those who initially formulated it were well-intentioned, it has recently been badly misused. Holmes cited as examples the labeling of the U.S. invasion of Panama as "Operation Just Cause" and the simplistic use of just war categories by U.S. officials in the Gulf crisis. "It does not . . . count against a theory that some people misinterpret or misuse it; but it does reflect on the serviceability of a theory . . . that it lends itself so readily to such abuse and can become an instrument for the rationalization of war rather than for its limitation, both in frequency and destructiveness." Regrettably, Holmes lamented, just war theory helps perpetuate the very thing it was meant to curb.

Just peace theory, according to Holmes, provides a needed corrective to much of the thinking on war and peace, particularly in terms of challenging people to think of peace as more than the absence of war and to recognize the central role of justice in the peace equation. Limiting consideration of peace merely to the absence of war often provides the soil out of which the next war will spring. "A refocusing of attention is needed, away from a near-exclusive preoccupation with war—when to fight it, how to fight it, and how to conclude it to maximum advantage for oneself—to a concern with how to design a peace which will serve the interests of all people" and make all the fixation on war unnecessary.

Holmes contended that one limitation of current just peace theory, as well as all other perspectives on war and peace, is that they do not reach far enough across religious and cultural boundaries. "No religious perspective on issues of war and peace has much hope of effecting serious changes in the world unless it cultivates common ground both with peoples of other religions and also with those who are nonreligious."

The "hermeneutics of suspicion" employed by Thistlethwaite in her critique of just war criteria was criticized by two participants for setting too rigid a moral standard. One speaker argued that it is not immoral to take an action that is justified by a universal criterion when that action also serves one's self-interest. Another contended that Thistlethwaite adopted an excessively conspiratorial view of how the war was conducted and how just war theory was misused. According to Langan, one can concede that the use of just war theory may have been disappointing or even objectionable without accepting that the theory was intentionally misused to serve evil purposes. It seems more likely, he argued, that honest people tried to appropriate the norms and apply them conscientiously, even though the results turned out to be unacceptable to the skeptics and critics.

In an effort to clarify the relationship between just war and just peace theories, Lintner explained that the just peace theorists do not contend that just war theory is wrong, merely that it is much too narrow. Those advocating just peace theory are attempting to widen the lens through which the religious community looks at issues of war and peace. If the debate is confined to the narrow lens provided by just war theory, it is an open question whether it does more harm than good. An additional problem is that the political community has appropriated the use of just war criteria to the point that policymakers draw their own conclusions about whether the criteria have been met or not, even when the religious community comes to a diametrically opposed conclusion.

A PACIFIST PERSPECTIVE

A pacifist perspective was presented by John Yoder, professor of theology at Notre Dame and a member of the Mennonite Church. While granting that the just war rhetoric can be useful for certain purposes, Yoder faulted the theory on several counts. Most fundamental is the fact that "the system predisposes its users toward a foreshortening of the ethical issues, in ways that lead people to forget the original presumption against harming the neighbor, which is the condition of the possible moral coherence of just war discourse in the first place." Moreover, just war thinking makes the faulty presumption that decisions regarding war are made at a particular time, when all the facts are at hand. But military decision making, like other political decision making, is a product of a process deeply influenced by "prior scenarios, negligences and commitments." For instance, the Gulf War was the product of a decade during which the West encouraged and armed Saddam Hussein. But this is the kind of information that just war considerations generally disregard.

Additional weaknesses of just war theory, according to Yoder, include the false presumption that the multiple criteria of the theory can be addressed with sufficient precision to approximate objectivity. Moreover, not all the facts can be gathered to reach valid judgments, especially when information is being so carefully "managed" by the governing power. Just war theory also permits the belligerent government to be both judge and executioner in its own conflict. Finally, the distinction between "intended" and "collateral" damage makes a mockery of the notion of "proportionality." "When more people (mostly children) are killed by bombing sewage treatment plants and cutting the electricity to hospitals than by bombing airfields, the concept of discrimination has become inoperative."

Yoder challenged the just war calculus because "the very notion of weighing incommensurables against one another is one initial mistake, and the set of tacit assumptions about who does the weighing is another."

The Gulf War illustrated a serious abuse of authentic religious values, he said, that has recurred repeatedly throughout history, which is that religion is called on to validate nationalist causes. Religion is frequently used to validate both sides of a dispute. "There is no more fundamental religious concern than the reflexive responsibility to prevent and denounce the abuse of religion. War always prostitutes religious language and institutions." In the case of the Gulf War this abuse affected Islam, Judaism, and Christianity.

Yoder contended that the religiously authentic response to the Gulf War or any war is to name and challenge the idolatry that war represents. Idolatry in the contemporary period "means sacrificing human lives to some creaturely value, namely to the interests of some ruling clique," which is the small ruling class that dominates every nation-state.

> What is at stake [claimed Yoder] is the commitment of the one true God (and derivatively, of the prophets and theologians who defined that interest, and the believers who confess it) to the entire human community, over against sanctifying any nation's designs. . . . Nationalism in that sense stands in contradiction to the authentic ideals of all the world's religions. That is what it means to be a world religion, rather than a tribal cult.

One can identify other forms of idolatry, but none, he said, is as serious as military nationalism.

God's uniqueness finds expression in the rejection of idolatry, seen in the sacrifice of human values to unworthy causes. It also finds expression in the affirmation of monotheism, which implies the unity of the whole human race. The theory of the nation-state, on the other hand, ascribes salvation in history not to God but to an oligarchy ruling over a single state, which is idolatrous.

Yoder carried this analysis one step further to argue that authentic prophetic monotheistic religion cannot affirm the sovereign nation-state at all. If there is one God, there are four things wrong with the sovereign state. First, the faith community itself is not the same as a nation-state. Second, the human community is not identical with or served by the nation-state. Third, "it is idolatry to sacrifice blood to any other value than the holy purpose of God." Fourth, any sovereign state is oppressive. It is dominated by a ruling minority, and it constitutes a regime rather than a government of, by, and for the people. Although democracies do better in sharing rule than do more oppressive forms of government, they are all various forms of oligarchy. In concluding this argument, he stated: "There is no theological legitimacy to the government of a sovereign national state if it uses the word 'sovereign' in a substantive way."

While the just war approach and other ethical approaches ask what is right and wrong in relation to war and peace, the most fundamental question that ought to be asked is, "What do these events mean under God?" Ethics is a very secondary consideration. "The needed vocabulary is sin, redemption, providence, presumption, repentance, reconciliation, sacrifice, not cost and benefit. Thus, to resituate the agenda, placing the cosmic and eschatological dimensions of the conflict above the moral ones, will not lead to neglecting the moral analysis, but will put it in a truer light."

The pacifist tradition, he said, is far from being a moralistic or legalistic fixation on the prohibition of bloodshed. Rather, it is the only view which recognizes that "most of the causes to which we are accustomed to sacrifice the lives of others are idols." In Yoder's view this position is not an idealistic or optimistic posture, but it considers enmity to be the fundamental human tragedy and redemption the central remedy. This position "makes peace at the cost of suffering." Moreover, it "proclaims a cosmic vision whose ultimate implementation is independent of the benevolence or the opposition of particular kings or emperors." Jesus provides the answer to the continuing pattern of revenge and retaliation, which seem to be universal norms and which generate so much of the world's violence.

In his response, Professor Richard Miller of the Department of Religious Studies at Indiana University sought to sharpen Yoder's argument that pacifists may use just war criteria for certain purposes. For Miller, the utilization of just war tenets presupposes that some wars can be justified, which is contrary to the pacifist position. Miller asserted that pacifists can use just war criteria on only two grounds.

> First, pacifists can refer to just war criteria to identify, when appropriate, the incongruities between political rhetoric and historical events, especially when that rhetoric invokes just war categories. . . . Second, just war criteria can be invoked in order to call attention to discrepancies between the principles of limited war and the actual practices in a specific

war, hoping to keep it from assuming the magnitude of a total war. In this way just war criteria can be used instrumentally by pacifists who seek to make the world less violent.

Miller reacted to the assertions of both Yoder and Thistlethwaite that just war criteria tend to overlook or to rationalize suffering in war. He argued that it is incumbent upon the critics of just war to assess the prospective effects of the *alternatives* to war, both in general and in the case of the Gulf War. As just war theory can rationalize sins of commission, so can pacifism or nonintervention equally be criticized for rationalizing sins of omission. Not to intervene in the Gulf crisis would have perpetuated circumstances implicating us in brutality, rape, and other moral atrocities. In addition, sanctions, as an alternative to war, take their own heavy toll, particularly among civilians, and may constitute a form of indiscriminate structural violence.

These considerations of the Gulf situation involve us in judgments about moral ambiguity, judgments that inevitably entail a mixture of justice and injustice. Miller contended that "one of the greatest casualties of the Gulf War was the loss of an appreciation for moral complexity." In place of a debate about complexities and ambiguities, the war became a test case for "either celebrating or condemning the theory of just war criteria." The debate ought to be casuistical rather than theoretical, and room ought to be provided for considerations of relative justice.

"Relative justice," argued Miller:

> should work to deflate appeals to what I have called American exceptionalism, the idea that Americans transcend the moral canons according to which other cultures should be evaluated. Seen in this way, relative justice ought to function, in part at least, as a counterideological criterion, reminding us that the language of saints and sinners is inappropriate when describing those involved in war, and preventing us from adopting a double standard when evaluating various practices in war. Relative justice ought to keep us sober and honest when assessing the justice of war, calling attention to the fallibility of human judgments and the limits of our moral visions.

But there is also another implication of relative justice.

> Relative justice is meant to remind us that just war criteria provide grounds for talking about *justified* actions only; it is not meant to imply that those collectivities who enter war protectively or defensively are

incarnations of political virtue. Relative justice suggests that it would be too heavy a burden to insist that third-party actors must satisfy conditions of righteousness as a prerequisite for defending a just cause. . . . Relative justice distills the sense of war's moral ambiguity, the fact that judgments must balance competing and conflicting verdicts when assessing the overall justice of war. . . . The task that remains is not to settle some grand, theoretical question about the merits of just war criteria, but to determine whether, on balance, one set of sins outweighed the avoidance of others.

What is required are casuists, not theorists. But Miller also granted, as Yoder would insist, that relative justice must also include what H. Richard Niebuhr, the Protestant theologian who taught at Yale, understands as "the tragedy and remorse, the acknowledgement of imperfection, that ought to accompany entrance into war."

Referring to Yoder's discussion of the sovereignty of the state being inconsistent with faithful monotheism, Professor Greenberg pointed out the strain of antisovereignty that is evident in the writings of some important Jewish thinkers. During World War II the leader of Orthodox Jewry, Jacob Rosenheim, saw sovereignty as the cause of the war and viewed the role of Judaism as promoting antisovereignty. It is accepted by all branches of Judaism that after the coming of the Messiah, sovereign states will disappear.

Elaborating on this point, Mirsky asserted that it can be accepted as a theological truth that states are fundamentally idolatrous, and yet faithful people can still work within states in ways to ensure that their religious values are not too seriously distorted. Certainly in the Jewish tradition one sees evidence of this tension between recognizing the state as evil and yet working within the state framework. One way that the Jewish tradition has mediated this tension is through the concept of covenant, which recognizes that the duly constituted political authority has a certain kind of legitimacy, but also recognizes that that legitimacy is contingent on states acting justly and righteously. This grants a provisional legitimacy to the state while leaving meaningful room for criticism and transcendence. The Jewish tradition also sees political sovereignty as only one kind of authority; priestly authority and rabbinic authority constitute other sources of authority.

Differing views regarding the legitimacy of political authority and the state may lie behind much of the debate about war and just war theory. Langan pointed out that differences over whether or not the state is idolatrous really reflect differences in politics. The Catholic view of just war in part derives from the fact that the "the Catholic assessment of the political is much more Aristotelian, much more inclined to say that it is a necessary and appropriate part of human life."

Others expressed doubts that pacifists, who are opposed to the conduct of any war under any circumstances, have anything to contribute to just war theory, since war by their definition is unjust. But a pacifist, Chuck Fager, defended his right to use just war criteria and to engage in the debate over whether the criteria are in fact satisfied in any particular case, even though he ultimately rejects the legitimacy of armed force. He asserted: "As long as they continue to take my tax money, I am going to claim the right to comment on such rhetoric on the part of those who are spending it." He feels comfortable assessing government action in terms of just war criteria when the government cites them to defend a particular war, if only as a kind of a cost-benefit appraisal. Thus, on one level of discourse, he feels competent to examine whether just war criteria have been adequately met in practice, even while at another level he continues to challenge the entirety of the just war theory and to reject war as an instrument of policy. Similarly, he feels competent and entitled to participate in the debate about how the just war criteria might be refined and improved for those committed to them, and he believes such engagement is legitimate.

A synthesis of these perspectives was attempted by Professor Wink, an advocate of nonviolence. He pointed out that many religious analysts are fed up with the misuse of just war theory, "but when we get down to analyzing what actually went on and what we disapprove of, we find ourselves having to use those same kinds of moral discriminations that have been called the just war tradition." In trying to move beyond the just war and pacifist stereotypes, Wink asserted that as a Christian community "we need to agree that war is wrong, that violence is wrong, that the Christian church cannot condone, legitimate, or sanction violence as a solution in international affairs. What Jesus proclaimed as the kingdom of God . . . is an order in which violence is radically repudiated. Now if the Christian church could agree that we are no longer going to use violence as a solution, that we cannot condone it, that governments will do what they will, but the churches will not serve as legitimators or cheerleaders for those kinds of actions, then it seems to me we can use just war criteria." However, he suggests they be renamed "violence reduction criteria" because there is no such thing as a "just war." *✗*

If a term like "violence reduction criteria" is used, Wink argued, then those who come from the peace church tradition or from a position of religiously motivated repudiation of violence could still bring moral discrimination to bear on the conduct of a particular war, saying: "This is not proportionate. This is going too far. This has exceeded the bounds of the mandate that you have given for yourself and your own actions." From this perspective, Wink concluded that Yoder was justified in using just war criteria despite his repudiation of violence. But this approach differs significantly from the just peace approach in that just peace principles are not criteria for moral discrimination, but rather ideals toward which we should move. The just peace ideals and principles are critically important, but they do not displace the need for criteria to judge what is happening in a particular context or conflict. *✗*

Examine both
— Just Peace ideals & principles
— Criteria to judge what is happening in a particular context

THE LARGER AGENDA

Throughout the discussion, various issues arose that, although they exceeded the bounds of the symposium's agenda, were nevertheless thought to deserve serious attention in the future. Participants emphasized that their debates about the finer points of just war theory, just peace theory, and pacifism did not come to terms with the larger issue of the glorification of violence that so pervades American society, as well as other societies. Yoder suggested that the debates over the morality of the Gulf War do not begin to inspire the same enthusiasm as Sylvester Stallone does to the American public's passion for bloodletting. What really ought to be addressed, he said, is the fascination with violence, not the niceties of difference between just war theorists and pacifists. A truly authentic just war theology and just peace theology would "spend more . . . time discussing Rambo and John Wayne and various forms of crusade and glorification of self-interest than . . . our topic."

Participants also reminded each other that the full range of religious opinion in the United States was not represented at this small gathering. A comprehensive consideration of religious perspectives on these issues would require not only the inclusion of representatives of other denominations and religious bodies, but also wider representation from those bodies that were present. For instance, the full range of Catholic opinion on the questions under consideration was not reflected by the small number of Catholic theologians and ethicists present. And the same is true for all other groups.

Turning to other issues that ought to be addressed, Miller argued that one of the major sources of dissatisfaction with just war theory is that it does not provide the kind of "thick sense of culpability" that some analysts desire when assessing something like the Gulf War. Those who are dissatisfied yearn for a rhetoric of social criticism that gives fuller expression to the sense of tragedy, imperfection, and remorse that many analysts feel. If just war criteria "are going to work, one thing that religion of the West might be able to provide is a thicker sense of agency, culpability, and solidarity, so that moral casuistry about war does not let people off the hook too quickly."

The workshop did not address in any detail possible alternatives to war and violence. Nonviolence was mentioned, but some participants wished that more time had been available to consider what it would mean to really embrace the alternative of nonviolence. Thistlethwaite concluded that any approach to conflict must be judged in part by the extent to which progress is made toward the establishment of a new set of institutions that can replace war. More creativity needs to be devoted to developing effective forms of economic and other sanctions. The development over recent years of conflict management and conflict resolution theory and techniques holds great potential and has been frequently endorsed by churches in discussions of international affairs. However, she asserted that these theories have had little impact on the way states conduct their international relations. She concluded that we must be continually open to inventing and embracing new options that can serve as alternatives to war and violence.

To assure that the just war criteria have been satisfied is not to assure that justice has necessarily been accomplished, and similarly, to debate just war theory is not to debate the larger justice issues. Langan pointed out that the Gulf War was a means of coping with a particular case of injustice, but it did little to bring about a more just world. The root problems of the Middle East were left largely untouched by the strategies and outcome of the Gulf War. "So we wind up in a morally dissatisfied situation. Moreover, we could say that if we were honest with ourselves about the way that Europe ended up after 1945, that was a morally unsatisfactory outcome." While Americans were able to tolerate the outcome of World War II, the "Poles and Czechs and a lot of other people had to live with it in a very painful way."

To embrace just war theory is not to conceive of war as morally good. "War is a great and terrible reality," Langan observed. "It is only imperfectly moralized by even the most scrupulous adherence to just war theory. It is in some ways a great roaring catastrophe, and I do not want to be seen to deny that while still working within the tradition of just war theory."

Jean Martensen, director for Peace Education of the Evangelical Lutheran Church of America, elaborated on this point by asserting:

War is a sign of disobedience and sinfulness. War is not intended by God. All human beings are made in the image of God, and they are precious and unique. Lutheran chaplains in the military with whom we have spoken have been among the most adamant of our members about war representing a failure of human imagination, a diversion of resources, in short, an incredibly sad undertaking.

She indicated that she shared the grief of the Muslim participants who had stated earlier that when the Kuwaitis were invaded, they were sad for them and when the Iraqis were bombed, they were sad for them as well. "What we tried to do in our church during this war was to pray for those whom our government said were our enemies. Not only did we pray for members of the coalition nations, we prayed for all the peoples of the Middle East throughout the whole struggle."

A consensus emerged that the interfaith character of the workshop provided an unusual opportunity for dialogue across confessional lines. The dialogue suggested ways that the different faith traditions could enrich their appreciation of the complex issues associated with war and peace. The participants encountered new ideas and deepened not only their mutual understanding but also their comprehension of their own faith traditions. For instance, Professor Thistlethwaite noted how helpful interfaith dialogue is in refining just peace theory. To hear what it means to create *shalom* based upon Jewish reflections is helpful, since *shalom* is the goal sought by just peace theory. Similarly, refinement of the theory can come from insights provided by Islam. Such interfaith dialogue may also generate a theory that can find resonance and support across a range of faith perspectives and traditions.

Participants expressed a desire for further opportunities for this kind of interfaith dialogue, both to advance the discussion of war and peace and to promote peace. For Christians, Muslims, and Jews to study the Qur'an under the tutelage of an imam and the Torah under a rabbi, and then study the New Testament, would contribute significantly to interfaith tolerance and understanding. Insofar as mutual ignorance and hostility among these three faiths are a continuing seedbed of war, efforts to promote greater mutual understanding can constitute a significant contribution to peace.

GLOSSARY OF TERMS

Aristotelian. Pertaining to the doctrines, conceptual terms and framework, and methods found in the thought of the Greek philosopher Aristotle (384-322 B.C.). In the context used here, it refers to Aristotle's view that human beings are, by nature, political creatures and naturally come together to form a "polis" or political community.

Casuistry; adjective *casuistical.* The application of ethical principles to difficult cases of conscience in order to determine the right or wrong causes of action within a particular context.

Eschatology; adjective *eschatological.* A branch of theology concerned with future or final things and events. In Christianity, for example, eschatology deals with such subjects as life after death, the last judgment and the end of the world, and heaven and hell.

Fatwa; plural *fatawa.* An opinion or judgment issued by Islamic *jurists.*

Halacha; adjective *halachic.* That part of Jewish law supplementing the scriptural law. Based on common custom as well as written and oral sources, the *halacha* has been elaborated for centuries and forms the legal part of the *Talmud.*

Harb. In the Islamic tradition, any war other than jihad.

Hermeneutics; adjective hermeneutical. The science of interpretation, especially the branch of theology dealing with the principles of interpretation of the Bible.

Jihad. A holy war waged on behalf of Islam and ordained by Allah (God).

Jurist. A person knowledgeable in law, such as a lawyer or judge.

Just war doctrine. See the Introduction to this book, pp. xxv–xxxiii.

Lurianic Kabbalah. The school of Jewish mysticism named after the sixteenth-century mystic and teacher, Isaac Luria, who said that creation was a process of contraction of God into Himself.

Munich. Refers here to the Munich Pact of 1938 by which Britain agreed to allow Nazi Germany to annex part of Czechoslovakia. *Munich* is commonly used as shorthand for the failed policy of appeasement by Britain and France in relation to Hitler.

Ontology; adjective *ontological.* A branch of metaphysics that deals with explaining why any being exists rather than does not exist.

Qur'an; sometimes *Koran.* The sacred book of Islam that contains Allah's (God's) revealed teachings to the Prophet Muhammad.

Sanhedrin. From 63 B.C. to the sixth century A.D., the supreme council of the Jews, responsible for religious, civil, and criminal justice and administration.

Shalom. A Hebrew word meaning literally "peace," but also having the connotations of peace with one's fellow human beings and the creation of a more just human community.

Sunna. The body of Islamic custom and practice based on Muhammad's words and deeds.

Talmud; adjective *Talmudic.* The authoritative body of Jewish tradition composed of collections of biblical interpretations.

Torah. The law of Judaism. *Torah* can refer either to the first five books of the Bible or to the entire body of Jewish law and wisdom.

'Ulama. The body of Muslim clerics (mullahs) trained in traditional doctrine and law.

Ummah. The Islamic community.

SUGGESTIONS FOR FURTHER READING

The following suggested readings will help to provide a fuller account of the complexities surrounding religious attitudes toward using force, including the development of moral limits on war. Several different perspectives are represented.

Bainton, Roland. *Christian Attitudes toward War and Peace.* Nashville, Tenn.: Abingdon, 1979.

Burns, J. Patout. *War and Its Discontents: Pacifism and Quietism in the Abrahamic Traditions.* Washington, D.C.: Georgetown University Press, 1996.

Decosse, David E., ed. *But Was It Just? Reflections on the Morality of the Persian Gulf War.* New York: Doubleday, 1992.

Geyer, Alan, and Barbara G. Green. *Lines in the Sand: Justice and the Gulf War.* Louisville, Ky.: Westminster/John Knox Press, 1992.

Hallett, Brien, ed. *Engulfed in War: Just War and the Persian Gulf.* Honolulu: Spark M. Matsunaga Institute for Peace, University of Hawaii, 1992.

Hoffmann, Stanley, and J. Bryan Hehir. *The Use of Force: Political and Moral Criteria.* Woburn, Mass.: Book Tech, 2000.

Johnson, James Turner. *The Holy War Idea in Western and Islamic Traditions.* University Park: Pennsylvania State University Press, 1997.

————. *Just War Tradition and the Restraint of War: A Moral and Historical Inquiry.* Princeton, N.J.: Princeton University Press, 1981.

Johnson, James Turner, and John Kelsay, eds. *Cross, Crescent, and Sword: The Justification and Limitation of War in Western and Islamic Tradition.* New York: Greenwood Press, 1990.

Johnson, James Turner, and George Weigel. *Just War and the Gulf War.* Washington, D.C.: Ethics and Pubic Policy Center, 1991.

Kelsay, John. *Islam and War: A Study in Comparative Ethics.* Louisville, Ky.: Westminster/John Knox Press, 1993.

O'Brien, W. V. *The Conduct of a Just and Limited War.* New York: Greenwood Press, 1981.

Russell, Frederick H. *The Just War in the Middle Ages.* Cambridge, England: Cambridge University Press, 1975.

Schlabach, Theron F., and Richard T. Hughes. *Proclaim Peace: Christian Pacifism from Unexpected Quarters.* Urbana: University of Illinois Press, 1997.

Sohail, Hashmi. "Interpreting the Islamic Ethics of War and Peace," in *The Ethics of War and Peace: Religious and Secular Perspectives,* ed. Terry Nardin. Princeton, N.J.: Princeton University Press, 1996.

Walters, LeRoy. "Five Classic Just-War Theories." Ph.D. dissertation, Yale University, 1971.

Walzer, Michael. *Just and Unjust Wars.* New York: Basic Books, 1979.

Yoder, John Howard. *The Original Revolution: Essays on Christian Pacifism.* Eugene, Ore.: Wipf & Stock Publishers, 1998.

———. *When War Is Unjust: Being Honest in Just-War Thinking.* 2nd ed. Maryknoll, N.Y.: Orbis Books, 1996.

Participants in the Symposium

Mumtaz Ahmad is an associate professor in political science at Hampton University in Virginia. He holds a Ph.D. in political science from the University of Chicago, has been a fellow at the Brookings Institution and the International Institute of Islamic Thought, and has consulted on Middle East and Third World development issues for a number of organizations, including the Brookings Institution, the Middle East Institute, the Center for Strategic and International Studies, and the American Enterprise Institute. He is an associate editor of the *American Journal of Islamic Social Sciences.* His most recent book is *State, Politics, and Islam.*

Abdurahman M. Alamoudi is the founder and executive director of the American Muslim Council. He is currently a Ph.D. candidate at the Centre for Islamic Studies of the University of Wales, writing a dissertation on "Muslims in America."

Mir M. Ali has been a professor in the Department of Urban and Regional Planning at the University of the District of Columbia for over twenty-two years. He has written extensively on current affairs in the Third World and is a regular contributor to the monthly *Washington Report on Middle East Affairs.* Recently, he has been a consultant with the United Nations Development Program and the United Nations Volunteer Program.

Dale L. Bishop is Middle East director of the Church World Service and Witness Unit of the National Council of the Churches of Christ. He holds a Ph.D. from Columbia University in Middle Eastern languages and cultures, specializing in Iranian studies. He has taught at Columbia and published numerous book reviews and articles on Islam, Iran, Lebanon, the Palestinian question, and on Christians in the Middle East. He is a member of the board of directors of the U.S. Interreligious Committee for Peace in the Middle East and is a contributing editor to *Christianity and Crisis.*

Chuck Fager handles mail for the U.S. Postal Service. He is a Quaker and a pacifist. He worked in the civil rights movement as a member of Martin Luther King's staff in Selma, Alabama, in 1965, and was a conscientious objector during the Vietnam War. He has been a congressional staff member and a freelance writer, authoring a wide variety of books and articles. He has published an independent Quaker monthly newsletter, *A Friendly Letter.*

Alan Geyer is professor of political ethics and ecumenics at Wesley Theological Seminary and is concurrently senior scholar at the Churches' Center for Theology and Public Policy. He is contributing editor to *Christian Century,* of which he was formerly editor, and *Christianity and Crisis.* His most recent book, with Barbara Green, is *Lines in the Sand: Justice and the Gulf War.* He was president of the Society for Christian Ethics and has served on the governing boards of the National Council for Churches, the Carnegie Council on Ethics and International Affairs, the Society for Values in Higher Education, and Ohio Wesleyan University.

Gershon Greenberg holds a Ph.D. from the Union Theological Seminary and is associate professor of philosophy and religion at the American University in Washington, D.C., where he was founding director of the program in Jewish Studies and Center for Study of Jewish Thought in America. The author of numerous chapters, articles, and book reviews, he is currently writing on modern Jewish philosophers and has a book forthcoming entitled *Holy Lands and Religious America 1620–1948.*

Robert Holmes is professor of philosophy at the University of Rochester. He holds a Ph.D. from the University of Michigan. His interests include modern philosophy, ethics, political philosophy, and social philosophy. He has written *On War and Morality* and edited *Non-Violence in Theory and Practice.* He was Senior Fulbright Lecturer at Moscow State University in 1983.

Robert C. Johansen is director of graduate studies and senior fellow at the Joan B. Kroc Institute for International Peace Studies and professor of government at the University of Notre Dame. He was president of the Institute for World Order in New York (renamed the World Policy Institute) and the founding editor in chief of *World Policy Review*. In addition to writing numerous articles in major newspapers and journals, he has written a number of books on global security, including *The National Interest and the Human Interest: An Analysis of U.S. Foreign Policy* and *Toward an Alternative Security System*. He has conducted research at Princeton and Harvard, has addressed the UN General Assembly on reform and innovation in peacekeeping, and is on the board of directors of the Arms Control Association, the Institute for Defense and Disarmament Studies, and the World Order Models Project

John Kelsay is associate professor of religion at Florida State University, where he teaches courses in ethics and Islamic studies. He coedited *Cross, Crescent, and Sword* and *Just War and Jihad*. He is currently working on a book entitled *Islam and War: The Gulf Crisis and Beyond*.

Father John Langan, S.J., is the Rose F. Kennedy Professor of Christian Ethics in the Kennedy Institute of Ethics at Georgetown University and senior fellow at the Woodstock Theological Center, where he has served since 1975. He holds a Ph.D. in philosophy from the University of Michigan. He entered the Society of Jesus in 1957 and was ordained to the priesthood in Detroit in 1972. His many essays and articles have appeared in a wide variety of books and journals; with William O'Brien he edited *The Nuclear Dilemma and the Just War Tradition*, and with Alfred Hennelly, S.J., he edited *Human Rights in the Americas: The Struggle for Consensus*. He has acted as a consultant and expert on ethics for the Chemical Bank and the U.S. Navy Corps of Chaplains.

Samuel W. Lewis became president of the United States Institute of Peace in 1987. He retired from the State Department in 1985, after thirty-one years with extensive service in Italy, Brazil, and Afghanistan as a Foreign Service officer. In his last post, he was U.S. ambassador to Israel for eight years and was a prominent participant in Arab-Israeli negotiations, including the Camp David Conference, the Egyptian-Israeli Peace Treaty, and U.S. efforts to bring the Israeli invasion of Lebanon to a peaceful conclusion. He had previously served as assistant secretary of state for international organization affairs, as deputy director of the Policy Planning Staff, and as a senior staff member for the National Security Council at the White House. Before coming to the Institute, he was diplomat-in-residence at The Johns Hopkins Foreign Policy Institute and a guest scholar at the Brookings Institution. He earned degrees from Yale and Johns Hopkins, and has been awarded honorary doctorates by six other institutions. He also spent one year as a Visiting Fellow at Princeton.

Jay Lintner is director of the Washington office for the United Church of Christ's Office for Church in Society. In 1991 he played an active role in developing the church's response to the Gulf War and to the Civil Rights Act of 1991. He holds an M.Div. and D.D. from Chicago Theological Seminary. His publications include *Peace Futuring, Empowering the Church in Society, The United Church of Christ Social Policy,* and "God's Unbroken Covenant with the Jews" in *New Conversations.*

David Little is senior scholar in religion, ethics, and human rights at the United States Institute of Peace. He is director there of the Working Group on Religion, Ideology, and Peace, which is currently conducting a two-year study of religion, nationalism, and intolerance. He was formally professor of religious studies at the University of Virginia and has also taught at Harvard and Yale Divinity Schools as well as a number of other colleges and universities. His most recent publications are *Human Rights and the Conflict of Cultures: Freedom of Religion and Conscience in the West and Islam* (with John Kelsay and Abdulaziz Sachedina) and *Ukraine: The Legacy of Intolerance.*

Jean Martensen is director for peace education of the Evangelical Lutheran Church in America. Formerly she was a researcher, writer, teacher, and civil rights worker. She holds a Ph.D. in social psychology.

James H. Matlack is director of the Washington office of the American Friends Service Committee (AFSC). Educated at Princeton, Oxford, and Yale Universities, he holds a Ph.D. and has taught at Cornell University and the University of Massachusetts.

He has held numerous leadership positions in the AFSC and traveled extensively for the AFSC in Central America, Indochina, and the Middle East.

Richard Miller is assistant professor in the Department of Religious Studies at Indiana University. He wrote *Interpretations of Conflict: Ethics, Pacifism, and the Just-War Tradition* and is currently writing a series of essays tentatively entitled *Cases of Conscience: A Study in Practical Reasoning*, which will include an assessment of the Gulf War.

Yehudah Mirsky is director of publications at the Washington Institute for Near East Policy. He holds a J.D. from Yale Law School, where he was an editor of the law review. He writes regularly for *The Economist* on politics and culture, and his essays and reviews have appeared in *Washington Monthly*, *Yale Law Journal*, *Jerusalem Report*, and *The New Leader*. He is currently working on a study of halachic responses to the intifada.

Charles E. Nelson is executive vice president of the United States Institute of Peace. Previously he was an executive with two international trading companies and The RAND Corporation's housing and civil justice programs. He has also worked as a senior staff member in the U.S. Agency for International Development and in a private consulting firm as a lawyer, manager, and administrator on economic and social development programs in the Middle East, Africa, and Latin America. He holds an A.B. from Harvard University and an LL.B. from Harvard Law School.

David Novak is the Edgar M. Bronfman Professor of Modern Judaic Studies at the University of Virginia. He has taught at Old Dominion University, the New School for Social Research, the Jewish Theological Seminary of America, and Baruch College of the City University of New York. He holds a Ph.D. from Georgetown University. He served for over twenty years as a pulpit rabbi and for three years as Jewish chaplain at St. Elizabeth's Hospital, National Institute of Mental Health in Washington, D.C. He is the author of six books, most recently *Jewish-Christian Dialogue: A Jewish Justification*, as well as numerous articles in scholarly and intellectual journals.

William V. O'Brien is professor of government at Georgetown University, from which he holds a Ph.D. His principal fields of study are international law and relations, with emphasis on legal and moral issues of war. Among many activities, he has served as Washington consultant for the Council of Religion and International Affairs, as president of the Catholic Association for International Peace, and as a consultant for the National Conference of Catholic Bishops' Committee on War and Peace. On a research grant from the United States Institute of Peace, he completed a book entitled *Law and Morality in Israel's War with the PLO.*

Brian F. O'Connell is program coordinator for Peace, Freedom, and Security Studies for the National Association of Evangelicals. He writes and speaks widely on the moral and ethical dimensions of foreign and defense policy and the role of the church in international affairs. He has worked as a freelance writer, an organizational consultant on international affairs, and as coproducer of *WorldView,* a public affairs television program. He is on the board of directors of the Episcopal Committee on Religion and Freedom, is a founding member of Christians for Solidarity with Christians in the USSR, and is secretary of the National Pro-Life Religious Council.

David Saperstein is is the director of the Religious Action Center of Reform Judaism. He is also an attorney and an adjunct professor in comparative Jewish and American law at Georgetown University Law School. His articles on political and social justice issues have appeared in the *Washington Post,* the *New York Times,* and many general and Jewish periodicals, and he has written or edited five books on social justice themes. He has chaired four national inter-religious coalitions and currently serves on the boards and executive committees of over thirty national organizations, including the National Association for the Advancement of Colored People, People for the American Way, and the Leadership Conference on Civil Rights.

David Smock is senior program officer in the Grant Program of the United States Institute of Peace. Previously he was executive associate to the president of the United Church of Christ, executive director of International Voluntary Services, vice president of the Institute of International Education, and held various positions with the Ford Foundation. He holds an M.Div. from New York Theological Seminary and a Ph.D. in anthropology from Cornell University. He is the author of several books, mostly on Africa and the Middle East.

Susan Brooks Thistlethwaite is a professor of theology at the Chicago Theological Seminary. She holds an M.Div. from Duke Divinity School and a Ph.D. from Duke University's Graduate School of Religion. She was ordained in 1974 by the United Church of Christ. She is on the board of directors of the American Academy of Religion and is on the editorial boards of *Theology Today* and *Prism*. With Mary Potter Engel, she recently edited *Lift Every Voice: Constructing Christian Theologies from the Underside*. Her other books include *A Just Peace Church* and *Sex, Race and God: Christian Feminism in Black and White*.

Walter Wink is professor of biblical interpretation at Auburn Theological Seminary in New York City. Previously he was a parish minister and taught at Union Theological Seminary. In 1989-90 he was a Peace Fellow at the United States Institute of Peace. He is the author of a trilogy, *Naming the Powers, Unmasking the Powers,* and *Engaging the Powers*. His other books include *Violence and Nonviolence in South Africa, Transforming Bible Study, The Bible in Human Transformation,* and *John the Baptist in the Gospel Tradition*.

John Howard Yoder is professor of theology in the University of Notre Dame and a fellow of Notre Dame's Kroc Institute for International Peace Studies. He served the Mennonite denomination in overseas relief and mission administration, in ecumenical representation, and in seminary education. He was a professor at Goshen Biblical Seminary from 1965 to 1984 and was its president from 1970 to 1973. His best-known writings on matters of war and peace are *The Politics of Jesus, Nevertheless: A Mediation on the Varieties and Shortcomings of Religious Pacifism, What Would You Do?, When War Is Unjust, He Came Preaching Peace,* and *The Priestly Kingdom*.